DATE DUE

D1115025

Careers in Focus

Animal Care

Ferguson Publishing Company
Chicago, Illinois

Copyright © 1998 Ferguson Publishing Company
ISBN 0-89434-267-3

Library of Congress Cataloging-in-Publication Data

Careers in Focus.   Animal Care
        p.   cm.
    Includes index.
    Summary: Defines the top eighteen careers in the animal care field in terms
of the nature of the work, educational or training requirements, ways to get
started, advancement possibilities, salary figures, employment outlook, and
sources of more information.
    ISBN 0-89434-267-3
    1. Animal specialists--Vocational guidance. 2. Animal culture--Vocational
guidance. I. J.G. Ferguson Publishing Company.
SF80.C27   1998   98-34990
636'.0023--dc21   CIP
                                                            AC

Printed in the United States of America

Cover photo courtesy Mug Shots/The Stock Market

Published and distributed by
Ferguson Publishing Company
200 West Madison Street, Suite 300
Chicago, Illinois 60606
312-580-5480
www.fergpubco.com

W-10

Table of Contents

Introduction

The careers listed in this volume of *Careers in Focus* represent some of the most popular and sought-after jobs in the animal care industry. Some careers, like pet sitters, are open to almost anyone with the right skills and plenty of determination; other careers, like zoo directors, are open to a very few people who have appreciable education and experience in the field. If you have an interest in animal care, these articles should reveal what kinds of opportunities are open to you and what you'll have to do to reach your goals.

General Information

Animal care involves the care and maintenance of animals, both wild and domestic. The animal care field includes the training and breeding of animals, as well as promoting their health and care. It also includes the entire range of actions taken by humans to protect and preserve wildlife and ensure their continued survival, such as the regulation of hunting and fishing and the establishment of zoos and sanctuaries. Another important part of animal care is educating other humans about animals and their needs; for example, naturalists educate the public in a general way while veterinarians educate pet owners about specific concerns.

Structure of the Industry

The animal care industry operates, in effect, on two levels. The first level is the care of pets, while the second is the care of wildlife. There may be some overlap between the two, but they are generally quite distinct.

Pet care is a rapidly developing industry in the United States, where new pet sitting and pet grooming businesses are opening all the time. Such businesses are becoming more regulated but still do not have very stringent certification or education requirements. They are open to enterprising animal lovers with good people skills and business sense.

Careers in equestrian management and veterinary science, among others, straddle the line between pet and wildlife care. The management of horses is hard to categorize because horses may be pets but may just as often be working animals. Horses are also unique animals that require more specialized care than your average cats and dogs. Veterinarians and veterinary assistants stand out because they do actually work with both pets and wildlife and also because they have to meet very stringent training and certification requirements.

People who care for wildlife are generally well educated and highly experienced. It is a such a competitive field that educational requirements are rising as zoos and wildlife refuges choose only the very best applicants to fill their job openings. As other applicants wait for positions to become available, many volunteer their time caring for animals or continue their education, thus raising standards even higher. This field is becoming particularly vital as wild animals and their environments are threatened with destruction.

Careers

The field of animal care offers a wide range of careers for those who take a scientific interest in animals, those who prefer a hands-on approach, and those who want to combine the two.

Animal breeders and technicians help breed, raise, and market a variety of animals, including livestock, pets, and zoo animals. They work in many different settings and capacities, from overseeing unskilled farm workers to reproducing species for zoos.

Animal caretakers, as the name implies, take care of animals. The job ranges from overseeing the day-to-day activities of healthy animals to caring for sick, injured, or aging animals. Daily animal routine usually involves feeding and providing drinking water for each animal, making sure that their enclosures are clean, safe, appropriately warm, and, if needed, stocked with materials to keep the animal active and engaged. Caretakers may be responsible for creating different enrichment materials so that the animals are challenged by new activities. They may assist veterinarians or other trained medical staff in working with animals that require treatment. Animal caretakers may also maintain the written records for each animal. These records can include weight, eating habits, behavior, medicines given, or treatment given.

Animal handlers are all the people who work directly with animals, from the caretaker of your local park's petting zoo to the activist who reintroduces wild animals to national parks. Animal handlers care for, train, and study animals in such places as zoos, parks, research laboratories, animal breeding facilities, rodeos, and museums. An animal handler's job involves feeding the animals, cleaning their living and sleeping areas, preparing medications, and other aspects of basic care. A handler may also be actively involved in an animal's training, and in presenting animals to the public in shows and parks.

Animal shelter employees work in nonprofit organizations. Their duties are similar to those performed in animal control agencies, which are run by government entities—city, county, state, or federal. Animal shelters and animal control agencies differ in their purpose and philosophy. Animal shelters, also called humane shelters, are usually dedicated to the protection of animals and the promotion of animal welfare. Animal control agencies exist to ensure that the safety and welfare of people and property are not compromised by animals. In recent years, animal shelters and animal control organizations have increasingly been working together. Some animal control organizations maintain shelter facilities or take animals to shelters for care and adoption.

Animal shelter employees perform a variety of jobs related to the welfare and protection of domestic animals. Most shelter workers care for small domestic animals, such as cats, dogs, and rabbits, but employees at some shelters may also work with horses, goats, pigs, and other larger domestic animals. Sick and injured wild animals are usually cared for by wildlife refuges and wildlife rehabilitation centers, not animal shelters.

Animal trainers teach animals to obey commands so the animals can be counted on to perform these tasks in given situations. The animals can be trained for up to several hundred commands, to compete in shows or races, perform tricks to entertain audiences, protect property, or act as guides for the disabled. Animal trainers may work with several types of animals or specialize with one type.

Equestrian management workers include a wide variety of positions such as farriers, horse breeders, horse trainers, judges, jockeys, stable managers, riding instructors, farm managers, racetrack managers, equine insurance adjusters, breed association managers, race association managers, and related business, sales, and marketing positions.

Naturalists educate the public about the environment and maintain the natural environment on land specifically dedicated to wilderness populations. Naturalists are usually given a specific title, according to their job tasks, but their primary responsibility is always related to preserving, restoring, maintaining, and protecting a natural or seminatural habitat. Among the related responsibilities in these jobs are teaching, public speaking, writing, giving scientific and ecological demonstrations, and handling public relations and administrative tasks. Naturalists work in private nature centers; local, state, and national parks and forests; wildlife museums; and independent nonprofit conservation and restoration associations.

Among the many job titles a naturalist might hold are wildlife manager, fish and game warden, fish and wildlife officer, wildlife biologist, and environmental interpreter. Natural resources managers, wildlife conservationists, and ecologists sometimes perform the work of a naturalist.

Park rangers enforce laws and regulations in national, state, and county parks. They help care for and maintain parks as well as inform, guide, and ensure the safety of park visitors.

Pet groomers comb, cut, trim, and shape the fur of all types of dogs and cats. They comb out the animal's fur and trim the hair to the proper style for the size and breed. They also trim the animal's nails, bathe it, and dry its hair. In the process, they check for flea or tick infestation and any visible health problems. In order to perform these grooming tasks, the pet groomer must be able to calm the animal down and gain its confidence.

Pet shop workers, from entry-level clerks to store managers, are involved in the daily upkeep of a pet store; they sell pets and pet supplies including food, medicine, toys, carriers, and educational books and videos. They work with customers, answering questions and offering animal care advice. They keep the store, aquariums, and animal cages clean, and look after the health of the pets for sale. They also stock shelves, order products from distributors, and maintain records on the animals and products.

Pet sitters visit the homes of pet owners who are on vacation or working long hours. During short, daily visits, pet sitters feed the animals, play with them, clean up after them, give them medications when needed, and let them in and out of the house for exercise. Pet sitters may also be available for overnight stays, looking after the houses of clients as well as their pets.

Veterinarians diagnose illnesses and disease in animals and prescribe treatment. They also perform surgery on animals, inoculate them against diseases, set broken bones, and advise the caretakers on proper care and feeding. Most veterinarians are in private group practices or self-employed.

Veterinary technicians are skilled assistants employed by a veterinarian. Although they do not diagnose illnesses, prescribe medication, or perform surgery, technicians do assist in these procedures. They keep records, take specimens and X rays, perform lab tests, dress wounds, and prepare animals for surgery.

Zoo and aquarium curators are the chief employees responsible for the care of the creatures found at these public places; they oversee the various sections of the animal collections, such as birds, mammals, and fishes.

Zoo and aquarium directors are administrators who coordinate the business affairs of these centers. Like all executives, they have diverse responsibilities. Directors execute the institution's policies, usually under the direction of a governing authority. They are responsible for the institution's operations and plans for future development and for such tasks as fund-raising and public relations.

Zookeepers provide the day-to-day care for animals in zoological parks. They prepare the diets, clean and maintain the exhibits and holding areas, and monitor the behavior of animals that range from the exotic and endangered to the more common and domesticated. *Aquarists* provide day-to-day care for fishes or marine mammals and birds in aquariums. They prepare diets; clean and maintain tanks, equipment, and plants; and monitor the behavior of animals in their care. Zookeepers and aquarists also interact with visitors and may participate in research studies or in training the animals.

Zoologists are biologists who study animals. They often select a particular type of animal to study, and they may study an entire animal, one part or aspect of an animal, or a whole animal society. There are many areas of specialization from which a zoologist can choose, such as origins, genetics, characteristics, classifications, behaviors, life processes, and distribution of animals.

Employment Opportunities

Animal care workers can find employment in a variety of settings. The most obvious are those solely dedicated to animal care: animal shelters, aquariums, breeding farms, grooming salons, pet shops, veterinary offices and clinics, wildlife sanctuaries, and zoos. Animal care workers can also find employment in other settings where animals live and work, such as farms, national and state parks, and private homes. Finally, certain animal care workers may set up their own businesses, and pet groomers and sitters may even work out of their own homes.

Industry Outlook

The animal care industry in general is expected to grow over the next several years. Those occupations related to pets have an especially promising outlook because pet ownership is on the rise and many owners are willing to invest substantial amounts of money in the care and grooming of their pets. The outlook for occupations related to the care of wild animals is less certain. Popular concern for wildlife is high, but public funding for park rangers and other wildlife caretakers is limited. Furthermore, competition for such jobs is very high and turnover is low, resulting in comparatively low salaries and few job openings. As in all fields, animal care jobs can always by found by people with the right combination of education, experience, and determination; unlike many other fields, animal lovers can often create their own jobs.

Sources of Additional Information

American Association of Zoo Keepers, Inc.
Topeka Zoological Park
635 Southwest Gage Boulevard
Topeka, KS 66606-2066

American Institute of Biological Sciences
Office of Career Service
1444 I Street, Suite 200
Washington, DC 20005

American Veterinary Medical Association
1931 North Meacham Road, Suite 100
Schaumburg, IL 60173-4360

American Zoo and Aquarium Association
Conservation Center
7970-D Old Georgetown Road
Bethesda, MD 20814-2493

U.S. Fish and Wildlife Service
1849 C Street
Washington, DC 20240

Animal Breeders and Technicians

	School Subjects
Agriculture	
Anatomy and Physiology	
Chemistry	

	Personal Interests
Animals	
Science	

	Work Environment
Primarily indoors	
One location with some travel	

	Minimum Education Level
High school diploma	

	Salary Range
$15,000 to $26,000	

	Certification or Licensing
None	

	Outlook
About as fast as the average	

Definition

Animal breeders and technicians help breed, raise, and market a variety of animals: cattle, sheep, pigs, horses, mules, and poultry for livestock; pets such as canaries, parrots, dogs, and cats; and other more exotic animals such as ostriches, alligators, minks, and many zoo animals. Technicians who are primarily involved with the breeding and feeding of animals are sometimes referred to as *animal husbandry technicians*.

In general, animal breeders and technicians are concerned with the propagation, feeding, housing, health, production, and marketing of animals. These technicians work in many different settings and capacities: they may supervise unskilled farm workers; serve as field representatives assisting in the sales of animals to customers; work in kennels, stables, ranches, or zoos reproducing species and breeds for other clients or their own organization; or work on their own on a particular breed of interest. The diversity of employment available for well-trained and well-qualified animal breeders and technicians makes this career extremely flexible. As science progresses, opportunities for these technicians should broaden.

History

Breeding animals has been part of raising livestock since animals were first domesticated. With the discovery of genetics, the science behind the breeding selection became more exact. Great shifts can be made in a species with genetically selected breeding programs. All domesticated dogs extend from a precursor to the modern wolf. So even though miniature poodles and St. Bernards have extremely different appearances and are seemingly incompatible, they are actually so closely related genetically that they can reproduce with each other.

Farm animals have been bred to increase meat on the animal, increase production of eggs and milk, and increase resistance to disease. Both pets and farm animals have been bred for appearance, with show animals produced in almost every domesticated species.

As regions specialized in certain breeds, organizations developed to recognize and register breeds, eventually developing standards for accepted breeds. Organizations such as the American Kennel Club establish criteria by which species are judged, and the criteria can be quite specific. For example, dog breeds have specific ranges of height, shoulder width, fur color, arch of leg, and such, and any dog outside the variance cannot be shown in competition. This is partly to ensure that the species is bred by trained and informed individuals, and to keep the breed from inadvertently shifting over time. Breeds, however, can be intentionally shifted, and this is how new breeds begin.

Until the end of the twentieth century, breeding was controlled by reproduction through mating pairs, whether through natural or artificial insemination. Recently, however, there has been a radical breakthrough in cloning, where the gene pool of the offspring remains identical to the parent cloned. Although this work is extremely costly and experimental, it is expected to change the range of work that breeders can do in reproduction.

Nature of the Work

Most animal breeders and technicians work as *livestock production technicians* with cattle, sheep, swine, or horses; or as *poultry production technicians*, with chickens, turkeys, geese, or ducks. Other animal breeders work with domesticated animals kept as pets, such as song birds, parrots, and all dog and cat breeds. Even wildlife populations that are kept in reserves, ranches, zoos, or aquariums are bred with the guidance of a breeder or technician. Each category of animal (such as birds), family (parrot), species (African gray parrot), and even some individual breeds within a category have technicians working on their reproduction if they are bred for livestock or domestic use. Within each of these categories the jobs may be specialized for one aspect of the animal's reproductive cycle.

For example, technicians and breeders who work in food-source bird production can be divided into specific areas of concentration. In breeding-flock production, technicians may work as *farm managers*, directing the operation of one or more farms. They may be *flock supervisors* with five or six assistants working directly with farmers under contract to produce hatching eggs. On pedigree breeding farms, technicians may oversee all the people who transport, feed, and care for the poultry. Technicians in breeding-flock production seek ways to improve efficiency in the use of time, materials, and labor; they also strive to make maximum effective use of data-processing equipment.

Technicians in hatchery management operate and maintain the incubators and hatchers, where eggs develop as embryos. These technicians must be trained in incubation, sexing, grading, scheduling, and effectively using available technology. The egg processing phase begins when the eggs leave the farm. *Egg processing technicians* handle egg pickup, trucking, delivery, and quality control. With experience, technicians in this area can work as supervisors and plant managers. These technicians need training in egg processing machinery and refrigeration equipment.

Technicians in poultry meat production oversee the production, management, and inspection of birds bred specifically for consumption as meat. Technicians may work directly with flocks or in supervisory positions.

Poultry husbandry technicians conduct research in breeding, feeding, and management of poultry. They examine selection and breeding practices in order to increase efficiency of production and to improve the quality of poultry products.

Egg candlers inspect eggs to determine quality and fitness for incubation according to prescribed standards. They check to see if eggs have been fertilized and if they are developing correctly.

Some poultry technicians also work as *field-contact technicians*, inspecting poultry farms for food processing companies. They ensure that growers maintain contract standards for feeding and housing birds and controlling disease. They tour barns, incubation units, and related facilities to observe sanitation and weather protection provisions. Field-contact technicians ensure that specific grains are administered according to schedules, inspect birds for evidence of disease, and weigh them to determine growth rates.

For other livestock, the categories are similar, as are the range of jobs. For nonfarm animals, the average breeder works with several animals within a breed or species to produce offspring for sale. Although there are ranches that produce a large number of exotic animals, and some stables and kennels that run full-staff breeding operations, most breeders for pets work out of their homes, with animals that they appreciate. There are also production shops, usually referred to as puppy mills, that produce pets for sale, but do so without much regard to the quality or well-being of the animals they are producing. Dismissed as unprofessional by established breeders and usually challenged by local authorities for quality of care provided to the animals, these are commonly not reputable enterprises, although they may be profitable in the short-term.

One area of animal production technology that merits special mention because of the increasing focus on its use in animal husbandry is that of artificial breeding. Three kinds of technicians working in this specialized area of animal production are *artificial-breeding technicians*, *artificial-breeding laboratory technicians*, and *artificial insemination technicians*.

Artificial breeding can be differentiated by the goal of the breeder: food (poultry and cattle), sport (horses and dogs), conservation (endangered species kept in captivity), and science (mice, rabbits, monkeys, and any other animals used for research). Breeders work to create better, stronger breeds of animals or to maintain good existing breeds.

Because of the increasing cost of shipping adult animals from location to location to keep the gene pool diverse in a species or breed, animal breeders have developed successful methods of shipping frozen semen to allow breeding across distances. For zoo animals such as the elephant, rhinoceros, and hippopotamus, this has allowed zoos to build their populations with good genetic diversity without the overwhelming difficulty of transporting a several-thousand-pound male over expressways to attempt breeding with a new female to which he may or may not be attracted. Because semen can be examined microscopically, the technician is able to eliminate problem samples before insemination occurs.

Artificial-breeding technicians collect and package semen for use in insemination. They examine the semen under a microscope to determine density and motility of sperm cells, and they dilute the semen according to standard formulas. They transfer the semen to shipping and storage containers with identifying data such as the source, date taken, and quality. They also keep records related to all of their activities. In some cases they may also be responsible for inseminating the females.

Artificial-breeding laboratory technicians handle the artificial insemination of all kinds of animals, but most often these technicians specialize in the laboratory aspects of the activity. They measure purity, potency, and density of animal semen and add extenders and antibiotics to it. They keep records, clean and sterilize laboratory equipment, and perform experimental tests to develop improved methods of processing and preserving semen.

Artificial insemination technicians do exactly what their name implies: they collect semen from the male species of an animal and artificially inseminate the female. Poultry inseminators collect semen from roosters and fertilize hens' eggs. They examine the roosters' semen for quality and density, measure specified amounts of semen for loading into inseminating guns, inject semen into hens, and keep accurate records of all aspects of the operation. This area of animal production is expected to grow as poultry production expands.

Whether the breeding is done artificially or naturally, the goals are the same. Cattle breeders mate males and females to produce animals with preferred traits such as leaner meat and less fat. It is desirable to produce cows who give birth easily and are less susceptible to illness than the average cow. In artificial insemination, cows are inseminated with a gun, much like hens, which allows for many animals to be bred from the sperm of one male. By repeating the process of artificial breeding for many generations, a more perfect animal can be produced.

Horse and dog breeders strive to create more physically and physiologically desirable animals. They want horses and dogs who perform well, move fast, and look beautiful. Longer legs and shinier coats are examples of desirable show traits for these animals. Temperament is another quality considered in reproduction and is one of the traits that a good breeder can work for, although it is not directly linked to a specific gene.

Some breeders produce many small animals such as mice, rabbits, dogs, and cats. These animals can be used in scientific research. For example, some laboratories raise thousands of mice to be used in experiments. These mice are shipped all over the world so that scientists can study them.

Animals raised for fur or skin also require extensive technological assistance. Mink farms, ostrich farms, and alligator farms are animal production industries that need husbandry, feeding, and health technicians. As the popularity of one species rises or falls, others replace it, and new animal specialists are needed.

For all breeders, it is essential that they keep track of the lineage of the animals they breed. The genetic history for at least three previous generations is usually considered the minimum background required to ensure no inbreeding. For animals sold as pedigree, these records are certified by some overseeing organizations. For animals being bred from wildlife stock, purity of the genetic line within a breed or species is required before an animal is allowed to reproduce. Stud books list the lineage of all animals bred within a facility. Pedigree papers travel with an individual animal as a record of that animal's lineage. Both tools are essential to breeders to keep track of the breeding programs in operation.

There are several ways to decide which animals should be bred, and some or all of them weigh into the decisions that the animal breeders make. The physical appearance and the health of the animal usually comes first; this is called mass selection—where the animal is selected of its own merits. If the animal has successfully reproduced before, this is called progeny selection. The animal can be bred again, knowing that the animal has produced desirable offspring previously. However, if that particular animal becomes genetically overrepresented in a generation, then the breeder runs the risk of inbreeding with the generations to follow. So the value of that animal's offspring has to be weighed against the need for diversity in parents. Family selection also determines the value of reproducing an animal. Some genetic diversity can come from breeding siblings of a good breeder, but it may not be enough diversity if the breeder is working with a limited stock of animals. Pedigree is the final determiner in evaluating a breeding animal.

Requirements

High school students seeking to enter this field will find that the more agriculture and science courses they select in high school, the better prepared they will be. In addition, courses in mathematics, business, communications, chemistry, and mechanics are valuable. Nine months to two years at a technical school or a college diploma are the usual minimum credentials for animal breeders and technicians. For the student who has only a high school education, the road to this career will be much more difficult. By working as a stable hand and gaining valuable practical experience, someone without a high school diploma might be able to move up. However, a high school diploma is almost always necessary to enter any technical education program beyond the high school level.

Many colleges now offer two- and four-year programs in animal science or animal husbandry where additional knowledge, skills, and specialized training may be acquired. Besides learning the scientific side of animal breeding, including instruction in genetics, animal physiology, and some veterinary science, students also take business classes that help them see the field from an economic point of view. With the increasing use of technology for breeding livestock and domesticated non-farm animals, a bachelor's degree becomes more important for succeeding in the field. Master's and doctoral degrees are useful for the most specialized fields and the careers that require the most sophisticated genetic planning. Higher degrees are required for potential teachers in the field, and the current work being done in cloning is done exclusively by people with doctorates.

Whether trained by experience, at an academic institution, or both, all new hires at major breeding companies are usually put through some type of training program.

Certification is not required but nearly all major companies have certification programs which can enhance earnings and opportunities.

Opportunities for Experience and Exploration

Organizations such as 4-H Clubs and the National FFA (Future Farmers of America) Organization offer good opportunities for hearing about, visiting, and participating in farm activities. Four-H sponsors youth breeding programs, allowing students to learn first-hand about breeding small animals for show. Other organizations, such as the American Kennel Club, sponsor clubs dedicated to particular breeds, and these clubs usually provide educational programs on raising and breeding these animals.

Other opportunities might include volunteering at a breeding farm or ranch, kennel or stable where animals are bred and sold. This will give you a chance to see the work required, and begin to get experience in practical skills for the job.

For at-home experience, raising pets is a good introduction to the skills needed in basic animal maintenance. Learning how to care for, feed, and house a pet provides some basic knowledge of working with animals. In addition, interested students can learn more about this field by reading books on animals and their care. But unless you have background and experience in breeding, and a good mentor to work with, it is not recommended that you start breeding your pet. There are literally millions of unwanted dogs and cats that come from mixed breeds or unpedigreed purebreds, and many of these animals are destroyed because there are no homes for them.

Other opportunities that provide animal maintenance experience include volunteering to work at animal shelters, veterinary offices, and pet breeders' businesses.

Methods of Entering

The most common ways of entering the field of animal breeding are through direct, on-the-job experience, by attending a two-year technical school or a four-year college, or some combination of the two.

Most available programs in animal production technology are relatively new, and many job placement procedures have not been developed to the fullest degree. However, many avenues are open, and employers recognize the importance of education at the technical level. Many junior colleges participate in "learn-and-earn" programs, in which the college and prospective employer jointly provide the student's training, both in the classroom and through on-the-job work with livestock and other animals. Most technical programs offer placement services for graduates, and the demand for qualified people often exceeds the supply.

Advancement

Even when a good training or technical program is completed, the graduate often must begin work at a low level before advancing to positions with more responsibility. But the technical program graduate will advance much more rapidly to positions of major responsibility and greater financial reward than the untrained worker.

Those graduates willing to work hard and keep abreast of changes in their field may advance to *livestock breeder*, *feedlot manager*, supervisor, or *artificial breeding distributor*. If they have the necessary capital, they can own their own livestock ranches.

Employment Outlook

Continuing changes are expected in the next few years, in both the production and the marketing phases of the animal production industry. Because of the costs involved, it is almost impossible for a one-person operation to stay in business for farm animals. As a result, cooperatives of consultants and corporations will become more prevalent with greater emphasis placed on specialization. This, in turn, will increase the demand for technical program graduates. Other factors, such as small profit margins, the demand for more uniform products, and an increasing foreign market, will result in a need for more specially trained personnel. This is a new era of specialization in the animal production industry; graduates of animal production technology programs have an interesting and rewarding future ahead of them.

For domesticated non-farm animals, breeders usually work with individual species and do so because they love the animals, not for a profit-bearing business. According to the American Kennel Club, the average dog breeder loses money on each successful litter.

Earnings

Salaries vary widely depending on employer, the technicians' educational and agricultural background, the kind of animal the technicians work with, and the geographical areas in which they work. In general, the salaries of all agricultural technicians tend to be lower in the northeastern part of the nation and higher in California and some parts of the Midwest, such as Minnesota and Iowa. According to the National Association of Colleges and Employers, starting salaries for animal breeders with a bachelor's degree averaged $24,900 in 1997. Salaries for technicians are significantly lower, ranging from approximately $15,000 to $26,000 a year or more. In addition, many technicians receive food and housing benefits that can amount to several thousand dollars a year. Other fringe benefits vary according to employer but can include paid vacation time, health insurance, and pension benefits.

Conditions of Work

Working conditions vary from operation to operation, but certain factors always exist. Much of the work is done inside in all types of facilities. Barns, pens, and stables are the most common facilities for farm animals; non-farm animals may be bred in private homes or housing facilities. Both types of work often require long, irregular hours, and work on Sundays and holidays. Salaries are usually commensurate with the hours worked, and there are usually slack seasons when time off is given to compensate any extra hours worked. But for people with a strong desire to work with animals, long working hours or other less desirable conditions are offset by the benefits of this career.

Animal breeders and technicians are often their own bosses and make their own decisions. While this can be an asset to those who value independence, prospective animal breeders and technicians must realize that self-discipline is the most valuable trait for success.

Sources of Additional Information

American Society of Animal Science
309 West Clark Street
Champaign, IL 61820
Tel: 217-356-3182

The following is a conglomerate of state and beef breed registry associations representing farmers, breeders, and feeders of beef cattle. It functions as the central agency for national public information distribution and legislative efforts and as the industry liaison for the beef cattle business. For more information, contact its national headquarters:

National Cattlemen's Association
PO Box 3469
Englewood, CO 80155
Tel: 303-694-0305

National Grain and Feed Association
725 15th Street, NW, Suite 500
Washington, DC 20005
Tel: 202-289-0873

U.S. Department of Agriculture
Human Resources Division, Agricultural Research Service
6305 Ivy Lane
Greenbelt, MD 20770
WWW: http://www.ars.usda.gov/

American Kennel Club
51 Madison Avenue
New York, NY 10010
Email: info@akc.org
WWW: http://www.akc.org/akc

National Association of Animal Breeders
PO Box 1033
Columbia, MO 65205

In addition to these organizations many animal breeds have their own representative organization that will provide information on the breed, as well as offer educational programs, provide a forum for discussing issues, problems, and trends with the breed, and offer networking opportunities for people looking to get started in working the breed.

Animal Caretakers

School Subjects

Anatomy and Physiology
Biology
Health

Personal Interests

Science
Volunteering
Wildlife

Work Environment

Indoors and outdoors
One location with some travel

Minimum Education Level

High school diploma

Salary Range

$8,800 to $15,000 to $26,000

Certification or Licensing

Required for certain specialties
(laboratory animal technician or
technologist)

Outlook

Faster than the average

DOT

410

GOE

03.03.02

Definition

Animal caretakers, as the name implies, take care of animals. The job ranges from the day-to-day normal activities for a healthy animal to caring for sick, injured, or aging animals. Daily animal routine usually involves feeding and providing drinking water for each animal, making sure that their enclosure is clean, safe, appropriately warm, and, if needed, stocked with materials to keep the animal active and engaged. Caretakers may be responsible for creating different enrichment materials so that the animal is challenged by new objects and activities. They may assist veterinarians or other trained medical staff in working with animals that require treatment. Animal caretakers may also maintain the written records for each animal. These records can include weight, eating habits, behavior, medicines given, or treatment given.

History

The concept of raising, caring for, and medically assisting non-farm or non-working animals is relatively new. The only animals, with few exceptions, that were kept by people were worked, such as plow-pulling oxen, or eaten, such as cattle, poultry, and pigs. The few examples of animals kept for pets are scattered accounts through history. The Egyptians kept cats as long ago as 3000 BC; cats were probably household pets, but perhaps they were also for religious purposes. Until immunizations and pest control became common, though, keeping animals in the house was unwise for health reasons.

Over the thousands of years that people have kept animals for use, they have learned how to care for animals in captivity. Successful early farmers understood that animals needed them to provide food, shelter, and a healthy environment in which to live. From these early efforts, people have learned more specific methods of providing for animals' needs. But the idea to use these skills on animals which provide no labor or food was not accepted until nearly the 20th century.

The first institution that specifically focused on the humane treatment of animals was the Society for the Prevention of Cruelty to Animals, founded in England in 1824. In the United States, the American Humane Association was founded in 1916 to work with the animals used in the war effort. But these organizations focused on helping labor and food source animals. The first law protecting animals in the United States was passed in 1873. But changes in animal treatment and rights were gradual throughout the first part of the 20th century. During the boom of the ecology movement in the late 1960s and early 1970s, public attention became focused on the rights and the needs of wildlife and domestic animals.

Rachel Carson's *Silent Spring* brought attention to the plight of hunting birds, and their rapidly deteriorating numbers. Pesticides such as DDT was dramatically reducing the population in the wild. To save birds such as the bald eagle, massive ecological intervention was required to clean up the environment, but breeding programs, shelters, and rescue centers would need to save individual birds to keep the population high enough to allow recovery.

Animals used in medical and chemical experimentation were also gaining advocates who helped create laws to protect them and begin to develop standards by which animals could be used in labs. As the public saw films and still pictures of the substandard or even abusive treatment of animals, particularly primates, in labs, they began to review treatment of animals elsewhere. Zoos, circuses, parks, and other institutions were used to replacing their animals with ones pulled from the wild. These institutions were soon under criticism about their pillaging of wild populations for healthy animals that wouldn't survive long in their care.

The institutions responded by improving facilities, nutrition, breeding programs, vaccination programs, and other forms of assistance that kept their animals healthier longer. Part of that improvement was increased staff. Also, as public interest in wildlife increased, there was an increase in the pool of volunteers that these institutions could draw on for labor.

With the push to conserve and protect species and maintain the populations in captivity and in the wild, programs such as rerelease programs for injured animals, rescue programs for threatened populations, zoo breeding programs, pet breeding and care programs, and sanctuary land for wild populations became much more prevalent. Many of these programs began and continue to be staffed by advocates, volunteers, and professionals who can all be called animal caretakers.

Nature of the Work

Animal caretakers, also referred to by several other names depending on their specialty, perform the daily duties of animal care, which include feeding, grooming, cleaning, exercising, examining, and nurturing the individuals in their care. These caretakers have titles such as *veterinary assistants, wildlife assistants, animal shelter attendants, laboratory animal technicians, laboratory animal technologists,* and *kennel technicians.*

Animal caretakers are employed in kennels, pet stores, boarding facilities, walking services, shelters, sanctuaries, rescue centers, zoos, aquariums, veterinary facilities, and animal experimentation labs. They may also be employed by the federal government, state or local parks that have educational centers with live animals, the Department of Agriculture in programs such as quarantine centers for animals coming into the United States, and the Centers for Disease Control laboratories.

Almost every one of these employers expects the animal caretaker to provide the daily maintenance routine for animals. The caretaker may be responsible for one animal or one species, or may be required to handle many animals and many species. A veterinary assistant is likely to encounter dogs and cats, with the occasional bird or reptile. A *wildlife shelter worker* works with the local wild population, so for much of the United States that means working with raccoons, skunks, porcupines, hunting birds, song birds, the occasional predator such as coyote or fox, and perhaps large animals such as bear, elk, moose, or deer.

Caretakers are responsible for some or all of the following tasks: selecting, mixing, and measuring out the appropriate food; providing water; cleaning the animal and the enclosure; changing bedding and groundcover if used; moving the animals from night facilities to day facilities or exercise spaces or different quarters; sterilizing facilities and equipment not in use; recording and filing statistics, medical reports, or lab reports on each animal; and providing general attention and affection to animals that need human contact.

The animal caretaker learns to recognize signs of illness such as lack of appetite, fatigue, skin sores, and changed behavior. They check the animals they can physically approach or handle for lumps, sores, fat, texture of the skin, fur, or feathers, and condition of the mouth. Since most animals do not exhibit signs of illness until they are very ill, it is important that the caretaker that sees the animal most regularly note any small change in the animal's physical or mental state.

The caretaker also maintains the animal's living quarters. For most animals in their care, this will be an enclosure of some type. The enclosure has to be safe and secure. The animal should not be able to injure itself within the enclosure, be able to escape, or have outside animals able to get into the enclosure. Small holes in an enclosure wall wouldn't threaten a coyote, but small holes that a snake can pass through could threaten a rabbit. The enclosures are designed to be safe for the animals, but also to make the animal feel safe. This means providing an enclosure that the animal feels it can guard; larger enclosures can make an animal feel that it cannot protect the space adequately, so it will pace relentlessly to try to control the territory. But inappropriately small enclosures can be just as damaging. If the animal cannot get sufficient exercise within the enclosure, it will also suffer both psychologically and physically.

Enrichment activities provide the animal with something to keep it engaged and occupied while in its home. For even the smallest rodent, enrichment activities are required. Most of us are familiar with enrichment toys for our pets. These are balls and squeaky toys for dogs and cats, bells and different foot surfaces for birds, and tunnels and rolling wheels for hamsters and gerbils. Wild animals require the same stimulation, which animal caretakers can provide by hiding food in containers that require ingenuity and tools for an animal such as a raccoon to work on, or ropes and innertubes for primates to swing on and play with.

Animals that can be exercised are taken to exercise areas and worked. For hunting birds this may mean flying them on a creance (tether); for dogs it may mean a game of fetch in the yard. Domestic animal shelters, vet offices, kennels, boarding facilities, and dog walking services will involve working predominantly with domesticated dogs and cats, and perhaps horses at boarding centers. Exercise often consists of walks or free runs within an enclosed space. The animal caretaker for these employers often works with a rotating population of animals, some of whom may only be in their care for a few hours or days, although some animals may be cared for over longer periods. Caretakers at sanctuaries, quarantines, laboratories, and such may care for the same animals for months or years.

It is, however, an unpleasant side of the job that in almost every facility the caretaker will have to deal with the death of an animal in his or her care. For veterinary offices, shelters, and wildlife facilities of any type, animal deaths are a part of everyone's experience. Shelters may choose to euthanize (kill) animals that are beyond medical treatment, deemed unadoptable, or unmaintainable because of their condition or the facilities' inability to house them. But even for places without a euthanasia policy, any center working with older, injured, sick, or rescued animals is going to lose the battle to save some of them. For the animal caretaker, this may mean losing an animal that just came in that morning, or losing an animal that he or she fed nearly every day for years. It can be as painful as losing one's own pet.

As an animal caretaker gains experience working with the animals, the responsibilities may increase. Caretakers may begin to perform tasks that either senior caretakers were performing or medical specialists were doing. This can include administering drugs; clipping nails, beaks, and wing feathers; banding wild animals with identification tags; and training the animal.

There are numerous clerical tasks that may also be part of the animal caretakers' routine. Beyond the medical reports made on the animals, animal caretakers may be required to screen people looking to take an animal home and write status reports or care plans. The animal caretaker may be responsible for communicating to an animal's owner on the status of the animal in his or her care. Other clerical and administrative tasks may be required, depending on the facilities, the specific job, and the employer. But for most animal caretakers, the day is usually spent looking after the wellbeing of the animals.

Requirements

Students preparing for animal caretaker careers need a high school diploma. While in high school, classes in anatomy and physiology, science, and health are recommended. Students can obtain valuable information by taking animal science classes, where available. Any knowledge about animal breeds, behavior, and health is helpful. The basics of human nutrition, disease, reproduction, and aging help to give a background for learning about these topics for different species. A basic grasp of business and computer skills will help with the clerical tasks.

There are two-year college programs in animal health that lead to an associate's degree. This type of program offers courses in anatomy and physiology, chemistry, mathematics, clinical pharmacology, pathology, radiology, animal care and handling, infectious diseases, biology, and current veterinary treatment. Students graduating from these programs go on to work in veterinary practices, shelters, zoos and aquariums, pharmaceutical companies, and laboratory research facilities. Students should look for programs accredited by the American Veterinary Medical Association.

Apprenticing for the handling of wild hunting birds is required by most facilities. This can include having apprentices pursue a falconry license, which means apprenticing to a licensed falconer. Licenses for assistant laboratory animal technician, laboratory animal technician, and laboratory animal technologist are available through the American Association for Laboratory Animal Science and may be required by some employers.

A bachelor's degree is required for many jobs, particularly in zoos and aquariums. Degrees in wildlife management, biology, zoology, animal physiology, or other related fields are most useful.

Animal caretakers should have great love, empathy, and respect for animals. They should have a strong interest in the environment. Patience, compassion, dependability, and the ability to work on repetitive, physically challenging, or unstimulating tasks without annoyance are essential characteristics for someone to be happy as an animal caretaker.

Opportunities for Experience and Exploration

Volunteering is the most effective method of experiencing the tasks of an animal caretaker. Most shelters, rescue centers and sanctuaries, and some zoos, aquariums, and labs rely on volunteers to fill their staff. Opportunities as a volunteer may include the ability to work directly with animals in some or all the capacities of a paid animal caretaker.

There is always a concern, sometimes justified, that an organization will never pay someone whose services they have gotten for free. You may not be able to get paid employment from the same organization for which you volunteered. But many organizations recognize the benefit of hiring prior volunteers: they get someone who already knows the institution, the system, and the preferred caretaking methods.

Volunteering also provides a line on your resume that demonstrates that you bring experience to your first paying job. It gives you references who can vouch for your skills with animals, your reliability, and your dedication to the field. Thus, you should treat any volunteer position with the same professionalism that you would a paid job.

Other avenues for exploration are interviewing people already in the position, or finding a paid position in a facility where animal caretakers work so you can see them in action. You may also begin by providing a pet walking or sitting service in your neighborhood, but be sure to only take on the number and kinds of animals you know you can handle successfully.

Methods of Entering

High school students who volunteer will be able to test the job before committing to it. They will also, as explained in the previous section, be able to get a job on their resume that demonstrates their experience in the field.

Two-year and four-year college programs offer some placement assistance, but familiarity with the regional market for organizations that use animal caretakers will assist you in selecting places to target with your resume. Many animal caretakers work in veterinary offices and boarding facilities or kennels, but animal research laboratories also hire many caretakers. Other employers include the federal government, state governments, pharmaceutical companies, teaching hospitals, and food production companies.

Advancement

Advancement depends on the job setting. There may be promotion opportunities to senior technician, supervisor, assistant facilities manager, or facilities manager. Some animal caretakers may open their own facilities or services. Services such as dog walking require little in the way of offices or equipment, so these are easy ways for animal caretakers to start on their own, with an established clientele that they bring from a previous position.

Laboratory workers can move from assistant technician to technician to technologist with increased education and experience. But for most promotions, more education is usually required.

Employment Outlook

The animal care field continues to expand. More people have pets, and are more concerned with their pets' care. Since most households have all the adults in full-time employment, animals are left home alone longer than in earlier times. Dog walking services, pet sitting and in-house care, boarding facilities, kennels, and such that provide assistance with the daily care of an animal for the working or traveling owner are far more prevalent and successful than before.

Veterinary services are also on the rise, with the increased number of pets, and the increased awareness on the part of owners that vet services are essential to an animal's' well-being.

There is a high turnover in the profession. This is due in part to the seasonal nature of some of the jobs, the low pay, and the lack of advancement opportunities in the field. Wildlife sanctuaries, release and rescue programs, shelters, and zoos and aquariums are heavily dependent on charitable contributions and fundraising efforts. Staff employment can be tied to the rise and fall of donations. Many of these institutions rely heavily on volunteer labor. As such, the competitiveness for the paid jobs is quite high.

Positions as animal caretakers in zoos, aquariums, and rehabilitation and rescue centers are the most sought after, partly because of the ability to work with exotic and wild species. Aspiring animal caretakers will find few openings in these facilities.

Graduates of veterinary technician programs have the best employment prospects. Laboratory animal technicians and technologists also have good opportunities. Increasing concern for animal rights and welfare means that these facilities are staffing more professionals to operate their labs. However, the criticism against the field and those who work in it can still be quite strong.

Earnings

Salaried employees earn an average salary of $15,000, according to the 1998-99 edition of the *Occupational Outlook Handbook*. These wages vary for the middle half of people employed in the field, from $11,440 a year to $19,670. The top 10 percent earn more than $26,000, but the bottom 10 percent earn less than $8,800 a year.

Self-employed animal caretakers who provide dog walking, kennel, sitting, or other cottage industry services do not have salaries that are readily available for review, but in large cities, boarding a dog overnight can cost $25 to $40, with a minimum of three dogs usually at one facility. Dog walkers charge between $5 and $12 a dog. There is little overhead for either service, beyond perhaps providing food.

Conditions of Work

Animals may either be kept indoors or outdoors, in any type of weather. Eagles don't come in from the rain, so animal caretakers caring for eagles still have to traipse outside to feed them when it's raining.

Depending on the facilities, heavy lifting may be part of the job. You may have to lift crates, animals, food, equipment, or other items big enough to accommodate a large animal. The work can sometimes be hard, repetitive, and dirty. Cleaning enclosures and disinfecting spaces can involve hot or cold water and chemicals.

The work can also be dangerous, depending on the animals you work with. Although animals that are handled correctly and are treated with the proper respect and distance can be quite safe, situations can arise where the animal is unpredictable, or is frightened or cornered. Although this is more likely with animal caretakers working with wildlife populations, large dogs, horses, and cattle are quite capable of injuring and killing people. There is a certain physical risk involved in working with animals, which may be as minor as scratches from nails or bites, but can be as great as broken or crushed bones, or accidental death.

Many facilities require long work days, long work weeks, odd hours, weekend work, holiday work, and intermittent schedules. Depending on the hours of the facility, the services provided, and the staffing, there may be several shifts, including a graveyard shift. Animal caretakers should be prepared to work a changing schedule. The needs of animals don't cease for weekends and holidays.

Also, for many facilities, animals that require round-the-clock care have to be taken home with an animal caretaker who is willing to provide whatever service the animal needs, including waking every two hours to bottle-feed a newborn chimp.

Sources of Additional Information

For information about animal laboratory work and certification programs, contact:

American Association for Laboratory Animal Science
70 Timber Creek Drive
Cordova, TN 38018-4233
Tel: 901-754-8620
Email: info@aalas.org

For information on programs in veterinary technology, contact:

American Veterinary Medical Association
1931 North Meacham Road, Suite 100
Schaumburg, IL 60173-4360
Tel: 847-925-8070 or 800-248-2862
WWW: http://www.avma.org

The professional programs of American Boarding Kennels Association include a facility accreditation program, a certification program for kennel operators, a complete staff training program, an ethics program, and publications for members, such as The Pet Services Journal and Boarderline (a newsletter).

American Boarding Kennels Association
4575 Galley Road, Suite 400A
Colorado Springs, CO 80915
Tel: 719-591-1113
Fax: 719-597-0006
WWW: http://www.abka.com

For information on the Student Career Experience Program sponsored by the U.S. Fish and Wildlife Service, contact the U.S. Fish and Wildlife Service, Office for Human Resources, in your state. You may also check their Web site at http://www.fws.gov/r9ohr/hp_scep.html

Animal Handlers

Agriculture Anatomy and Physiology Biology	School Subjects
Entertaining/Performing The Environment Wildlife	Personal Interests
Indoors and outdoors Primarily one location	Work Environment
High school diploma	Minimum Education Level
$16,000 to $28,800 to $41,600	Salary Range
Voluntary	Certification or Licensing
About as fast as the average	Outlook

Definition

Anybody who works directly with animals, from the caretaker of your local park's petting zoo, to the activist who reintroduces wild animals to national parks, is an *animal handler*. Animal handlers care for, train, and study animals in such places as zoos, parks, research laboratories, animal breeding facilities, rodeos, and museums. An animal handler's job involves feeding the animals, cleaning their living and sleeping areas, preparing medications, and other aspects of basic care. A handler may also be actively involved in an animal's training, and in presenting animals to the public in shows and parks.

History

From the old *stable hand* of the nineteenth-century Wild West to today's *horse trainer* for a movie western, animal handlers have long been in great demand. As long as animals have walked the earth alongside humans, society has invented ways to use animals for work, recreation, and research. Ancient Egyptian records of veterinary medicine date as far back as 2000 BC. Animal medicine was considered as important as human medicine, because of the great importance animals played in transportation and production. But animals weren't just admired for their practicality; people have always held affection and fascination for animals. The domestication of animals began during the Stone Age, and zoo keeping can be traced back to the twelfth century BC. Egypt, Greece, and China all have early records of exotic animals kept in collections for admiration and competition. Though many of the earliest zoos were kept only for kings and queens, public zoos have been in existence for over two centuries. The French Revolution resulted in the Jardin de Plantes in Paris going public and becoming a model for all the zoos to follow as monarchies fell around the world.

With the development of engines and motors over the last century, the role of animals in society has changed. Though seeing-eye dogs, laboratory primates, police horses, and canine patrol dogs are still put to work to aid humans, animals today entertain and fascinate more often than perform duties. Protecting animals has become an important aspect of every animal handler's job. For over one hundred years, government agencies have been in place to ensure the humane treatment of animals. The first such agency in the United States was chartered in 1866; it was the still-active American Society for the Prevention of Cruelty to Animals (ASPCA).

Nature of the Work

Wrangling an iguana for a movie production; preparing the diet for a zoo's new albino alligator; comforting bison to keep them from committing "suicide"; training cats for an animal-assisted therapy program at a nursing home. All these responsibilities, strange as they may seem, actually exist for some animal trainers. Many western states have long telephone book listings of animal handlers who rent out trained iguanas, horses, cougars, cattle, and other animals for movie productions. Zoos and marine animal parks hire highly trained keepers to feed, shelter, and protect some of the most exotic animals in the world. Bison, if not properly prepared for transport, can easily be provoked to stampede, sometimes killing themselves. And even cats are therapists these days, as people introduce their pets to elderly and ill patients who respond well to interaction with animals.

Whether taking on jobs like those listed above or working for a small park or large zoo, all animal handlers are called upon for the daily care and safety of animals. They may have special training in a particular animal or breed or work with a variety of animals. Jennifer Gales works in the petting zoo of Knotts Berry Farm in California, caring for the goats, ponies, rabbits, tortoises, and other animals visited every day. It is her responsibility to check the health of the animals, and to feed and water them. "You have to learn as much as you can about the animal's habits and personality," she says. "Every animal is different." With a wide knowledge of an animal's nutritional and exercise requirements, animal handlers make sure the animals in their care are well-fed, well-groomed, and healthy. They prepare food and formulas, which may include administering medications. Maintaining proper shelters for animals requires cleaning the area, ensuring good ventilation, and providing proper bedding. Animal handlers arrange for vaccinations, as well as look for diseases in their animals. They also prepare animals for transport, knowing how to use muzzles and kennels, and how to calm an animal. But an animal handler needs a rapport with the two-legged creatures as well; working with people is an important aspect of most animal care jobs, as many of these animals are kept for presentation and performance.

"Every day is different," Jennifer says, "because animals have good and bad days, just like people. There are days they just don't want to be touched at all, and they let you know it by their actions." The relationship between an animal and its handler can be very strong, particularly in training situations. Dogs trained for a police unit require specially certified trainers, and the dogs often both live and work alongside the officers to whom they are assigned. The same is true of handlers who train seeing-eye dogs or hearing-ear dogs; it is the handler's responsibility to train the animal to think of itself and its owner as one unit, thereby assuring it will watch out for both its own safety and that of its owner. Handlers who breed animals are often very devoted to the animals they place in other homes—they often interview prospective buyers, making sure the animal will have proper shelter, exercise, and feeding. Handlers who prepare animals for research in a lab must pay close attention to animal health, as well as their own; many states require health tests and immunizations of people who run the risk of catching diseases or illnesses from the animals they study.

Requirements

Take biology, chemistry, and other science courses offered by your high school. The study of science will be important to any student of animals, as will the study of psychology and sociology. Knowing about animal nutrition, health, behavior, and biology will help you to understand the animals you care for, and how to best provide for them. And if you do choose to go on to college, most animal-related courses of study are science based.

Some of you may think of animal handlers as people who spend all their time separate from the rest of the community, communicating only with animals and limiting interaction with humans. However, nothing could be further from the truth—most animal handlers work actively with the public; they present the animals in zoos and public programs, and may even perform with the animals. Join your speech and debate team, or your drama club, to prepare for speaking in front of groups of people.

Because so many animal programs, from petting zoos to animal-therapy programs, rely on community support, there are many volunteer opportunities for high school students looking to work with animals. Zoos, parks, and museums need volunteers, as do kennels, shelters, and local chapters of the Humane Society. These organizations may even offer students paid part-time positions. If few opportunities exist in your area, check with the nearest zoo about summer internship programs for high school students.

Though Jennifer Gales doesn't have a college degree, some of her coworkers at the Knotts Berry Farm petting zoo are pursuing degrees in the veterinary sciences. The value of a college degree depends on the work you do. Many animal handlers do not have degrees, but zoos often prefer to hire people with a postsecondary education. A degree can often determine promotions and pay raises among the workers of a zoo. Many universities offer degrees in animal sciences, zoology, and zoological sciences. There are also graduate degrees in zoology, which may require courses in physiology, animal behavior, and oceanography. Courses for animal science programs generally focus on animal research, but some programs allow students to create their own course plans to involve hands-on experience as an animal handler. The Santa Fe Community College in Gainesville, Florida, offers a unique and popular zoo animal technology program; students work toward an associate's degree while gaining a great deal of first-hand zoo experience. The students run an 85-species zoo entirely on their own and, upon graduation, enter bachelor's programs or other animal care jobs.

Some consider a job as an animal handler an internship in and of itself; after gaining experience in a petting zoo or teaching zoo, or working with a breeder or stable hand, some animal handlers pursue careers as zoo keepers, veterinarians, and animal researchers. Most college animal science and zoology programs offer some hands-on experience with animals; in the case of the Santa Fe Community College mentioned above, an internship with the school's zoo is required along with the academic classes.

Many unpaid internships are available for those willing to volunteer their time to researchers and other animal professionals. Check with your local university and zoo to find out about opportunities to study animals in the wild, or to reintroduce animals to their native habitats.

Some animal handlers in very specialized situations, such as patrol dog trainers and lab animal technicians, are required to pursue certification. The American Association for Laboratory Animal Sciences offers certification for those working with lab animals. But for the majority of animal handlers, no certification program exists. Accreditation is generally only required of the institutions and programs that hire animal handlers. The American Zoo and Aquarium Association offers accreditation, as well as memberships to individuals. Though members are required to have a certain amount of experience, membership is not mandatory for those working with animals.

"I have always had a love for animals," Jennifer says. "The only ones I don't like are snakes—I need legs on animals." It is important for animal handlers to love the animals they care for. What might not be as apparent, however, is the need for animal handlers to enjoy working with people as well. Animal handlers are often required to present the animals to park and zoo visitors, and to serve as tour guides; they also work as instructors in zoo and museum education programs. Some animal handlers even perform alongside their trained animals in theme parks and shows. Some shows, such as marine animal shows can be particularly strenuous, calling for very athletic trainers.

Working with animals on a daily basis requires patience and calmness since animals faced with unfamiliar situations are easily frightened. Animal handlers must be very knowledgeable about the needs and habits of all the animals in their care. Handlers are often called upon to transport animals, and they must know ways to best comfort them. Impatience may result in serious injury to both the animal and the handler.

Opportunities for Experience and Exploration

If you grew up with a family pet or have spent time on a farm, you're probably already very familiar with how to care for animals. But if you want to gain experience handling a large group of animals, contact your local zoo about volunteer or part-time positions. Many zoos have programs in place to introduce young people to the duties and responsibilities of an animal handler. If your local zoo doesn't have such a program, try to create your own: contact zoo keepers, express your interest in their work, and ask to "shadow" them for a few days.

Many part-time jobs are available to high school students interested in working with animals. Pet shops, petting zoos, stables, and kennels are likely to have a few after-school positions. In larger cities, you may be able to start your own animal care business as a dog-walker or pet-sitter. Or look under "animal handler" in the local telephone book. Some animal handlers work exclusively with movie production crews and other entertainment venues; you may be able to work as a temporary assistant on a production.

Methods of Entering

Jennifer found it very easy to get her job with Knotts Berry Farm. "If you love animals," she said, "it just shows in what you say, and the way you talk about them. My interview was about an hour of me sitting there talking about animals." Depending on the area of animal care in which you want to work, you may be able to find many great opportunities. A high school job or internship is a good start; experience with animals is what is most important to employers hiring handlers. Any volunteering you've done will also look good to an employer because it shows that you have a personal dedication to the care of animals. Kennels, petting zoos, museums, and animal shelters often run classified ads in the newspaper; due to the lower pay and some of the hazards involved in handling animals, those positions are frequently available.

Jobs with zoos in major cities, or with animal shows, can be highly competitive. If you're hoping to work in a larger, more famous zoo, you should first pursue experience with a smaller zoo. Jobs working with marine mammals are also difficult to get; because there are few marine animal shows in the country (such as those performed at the Sea Worlds), you may first have to pursue experience with internships and college programs.

Advancement

Most people who work with animals are not looking to climb any ladder of advancement. As a matter of fact, many people change from high-paying careers to lower-paying animal care jobs just to do something they love. Much of the student body of the animal tech program at Santa Fe Community College is composed of people over thirty years old who have tried other careers. Some who have gained experience handling and training animals may start their own businesses, perhaps building their own stables of trained "actors" to hire out for area movie shoots, stage shows, parades, and other performances. Some animal handlers may pursue higher education while working full- or part-time, taking courses towards veterinary sciences degrees, or degrees in biology. With a degree, an animal handler may have a better chance at the higher paying, supervisory zookeeper positions. After years with a particular zoo, an animal handler can take on more responsibility and make decisions that influence the direction of the zoo.

Employment Outlook

With the popularity of cable channels such as the Discovery Channel and Animal Planet, as well as television specials and videos featuring animals, the public's interest in animals is only likely to increase. Zoos, parks, and museums will benefit a great deal from any increased exposure the public has to the animal kingdom. Zoos must also compete with television as family entertainment, and therefore are constantly thriving to improve their facilities with more exotic animals, better shelters, and more programs to involve the public directly with animals.

Concerns about the treatment of animals will perhaps lead to more stringent laws and certification requirements. Some activists hope to end the capture of animals for display in zoos; some even object to filming animals in the wild. But zoos are likely continue to operate and expand, with zoo professionals arguing that zoo animals are often safer and receive better care than they would in their natural habitats.

Earnings

The opportunity to work directly with a variety of different animals is often reward enough for animal handlers. Someone who owns a stable of well-trained animals used in performances may be able to negotiate for large contracts, or a successful dog breeder may make a comfortable living with an established business, but most animal handlers make do with small salaries and hourly wages. The Santa Fe Community College advises the graduates of their animal technology program to expect between $16,000 and $19,000 annually. This wage varies according to region—in the colder Midwestern and Northern states, and in California, animal handlers can make more than those living in the Southeast. An experienced animal handler may draw an hourly wage of $16 to $20. Many full-time, salaried zoo positions include health benefits.

Conditions of Work

Depending on the lives of the animals for which they care, handlers usually work both indoors and outdoors. But the indoors is often nothing more than an animal shelter, and not much different from the pens outdoors. Be prepared for smelly, messy, and dusty environments; if you have allergies, they'll be under constant assault. It will be both to your benefit, and the animal's, to make sure you work in well-ventilated areas. Some institutions, particularly animal research labs, require handlers to have immunizations and physicals before working with the animals. In addition to allergies, there is some danger of diseases transferred from animals to humans. These risks can be lessened with protective clothing like lab coats, gloves, and ventilated hoods.

The temperament of your animals will also effect your work environment. Handlers must be prepared for occasional scratches, bites, and kicks from animals with even the best dispositions. Though some animals can be very noisy when disturbed, handlers attempt to keep their animals' surroundings quiet and calm.

Sources of Additional Information

For general information about zoos, aquariums, oceanariums, and wildlife parks, contact:

American Zoo and Aquarium Association
7970-D Old Georgetown Road
Bethesda, MD 20814-2493
Tel: 301-907-7777
WWW: http://www.aza.org

For information on their zoo animal technology program, and other career information, contact:

Santa Fe Community College
3000 NW 83rd Street
Gainesville, FL 32606
Tel: 352-395-5604
WWW: http://www.aazk.ind.net/aazk/SantaFe.html

Animal Shelter Employees

School Subjects

Biology
Mathematics
Science
Speech

Personal Interests

Animals
Business management
The Environment
Teaching
Wildlife

Work Environment

Primarily indoors
Primarily one location

Minimum Education Level

High school diploma

Salary Range

$9,500 to $17,100 to $150,000

Certification or Licensing

Required for certain specialties:
Humane Investigator

Outlook

Faster than the average

Definition

Animal shelter employees work in nonprofit organizations. Their duties are similar to those performed in animal control agencies, which are run by government entities—city, county, state, or federal. Animal shelters and animal control agencies differ in their purpose and philosophy. Animal shelters, also called humane shelters, are usually dedicated to the protection of animals and the promotion of animal welfare. Animal control agencies exist to ensure that the safety and welfare of people and property are not compromised by animals. In recent years, animal shelters and animal control organizations have increasingly been working together. Some animal control organizations maintain shelter facilities or take animals to shelters for care and adoption.

Animal shelter employees perform a variety of jobs related to the welfare and protection of domestic animals. Most shelter workers care for small domestic animals, such as cats, dogs, and rabbits, but employees at some shelters may also work with horses, goats, pigs, and other larger domestic animals. Sick and injured wild animals are usually cared for by wildlife refuges and wildlife rehabilitation centers, not animal shelters.

History

The precursors of today's animal shelter employees were the pound masters of the colonial United States. In the early 1700s, animal pounds were built to house stray animals. Pound masters kept the strays until their owners claimed them. Animals that were not claimed were drowned or otherwise destroyed. In the eighteenth and early nineteenth centuries, the treatment of animals in the United States was frequently harsh and even cruel.

The first American Society for the Prevention of Cruelty to Animals was founded in 1866 through the efforts of philanthropist Henry Bergh and other early crusaders for animal welfare. Not long after, Caroline Earle White and the Women's SPCA of Pennsylvania founded the first truly humane animal shelter. These two events brought into existence the position of animal shelter worker as we know it today. As a result of these developments, the focus of animal shelter employees turned from animal control toward a greater concern for the welfare and humane treatment of animals.

The job of animal shelter employee took on another dimension in the middle of the twentieth century. Greater emphasis was placed on training shelter workers in better techniques of caring for animals, and better methods for humanely euthanizing (killing) animals were developed.

New positions for animal shelter workers are evolving as we move into the twenty-first century. Shelter employees focus on reuniting lost pets with their owners, adoption efforts, and humane education, volunteer, and community outreach programs. Studies now show that there is a strong link between violence toward animals and violence toward people. Environmental groups are educating the public about the interrelationships among plants, animals, people, and the planet as a whole. As public awareness of animals' importance and connection to mankind grows, the work of animals shelter employees will continue to evolve.

Nature of the Work

The duties of shelter employees range from cleaning cages and grooming animals to education, fund-raising, and business management. The functions a specific worker performs frequently depend on the size of the animal shelter. In a large shelter, duties are more specialized, and there may be a large staff to accomplish them. In a small shelter, a few individuals may be responsible for nearly all of the functions that are performed. Whatever the specific duties of an animal shelter worker may be, the goal is always to promote the welfare of animals.

Kennel attendants (also called *kennel workers*) generally tend to the animals' physical needs, such as feeding, exercising, and cleaning of living quarters. Of all shelter staff, the kennel attendants work most closely with the shelter animals, and an important part of their job is nurturing the animals through caring handling. In some shelters, kennel attendants receive animals that are brought in by their owners or by a humane investigator. The receiving attendant may be responsible for checking the general health of the new animal, finding an appropriate habitat for it in the shelter, and referring it for medical treatment when necessary. Kennel attendants keep records, such as the identification of the animal, size, weight, and general condition. More experienced or skilled kennel attendants may be trained to give some inoculations and perform euthanasia under the supervision of a veterinarian. Kennel attendants sometimes act as adoption counselors.

Adoption counselors screen applicants who wish to adopt animals from the shelter. They interview applicants to ascertain whether they will provide a good, caring home for an animal. An adoption counselor asks questions, listens carefully, communicates tactfully with people, and judges character. If the counselor decides the applicant is a good potential pet owner, he or she must try to match the qualified owner with an appropriate animal. If the adoption counselor believes a proposed adoption would not be in the animal's interest, the application is denied. A skilled counselor may be able to suggest a different animal that would be a better match for the applicant's situation. The adoption counselor puts the animal's welfare foremost, but also promotes the public image of the shelter.

Humane investigators (also known as *cruelty investigators* or *animal treatment investigators*) follow up on reports of animal abuse and neglect. They interview any witnesses as well as animal owners who are accused of mistreatment. If the cruelty investigator determines that abuse or neglect exists, he or she may issue a warning, call the police to arrest the individual, or confiscate the animal. Humane investigators respond to reports of abandoned, stray, or injured animals, and they free trapped animals. They transport rescued animals to the shelter.

Humane educators work at the shelter and in the community teaching about humane treatment of animals and raising awareness of other animal-related issues. They travel to grade schools, high schools, clubs, and other community organizations. They lecture about animal care and treatment, animal rights, the overpopulation problem and potential solutions, the relationship between violence to animals and violence to people, and the roles of the individual and the community in effecting change. Humane educators arrange tours of the animal shelter for interested groups, distribute printed educational materials, and inform people about other resources for humane education. Nearly half of the fifty states now require humane education in schools.

Shelter managers (also called *kennel managers* or *kennel supervisors*) oversee all the daily operations of the shelter itself. They hire and train kennel attendants, make schedules for staff and volunteers, evaluate work performance, and provide continuing education opportunities to improve job performance. Shelter managers supervise and/or perform the maintenance of the property, buildings, vehicles, and euthanasia equipment. In some shelters, the manager is responsible for operating the euthanasia equipment when animals must be destroyed according to shelter policy.

Shelter administrators are responsible for the overall operation of the shelter, its departments, and its programs. They select and hire shelter managers, humane educators, humane investigators, and department heads, and they may be in charge of personnel. Administrators advocate for the shelter by holding interviews with the media, fund-raising, attending community events, and recruiting new members. Shelter administrators must work well with people, and they must be good business managers. According to Doug Trowbridge, Program Coordinator for Field Services of the American Humane Association (AHA), the majority of animal shelters that fail in the United States are forced to close because they were not run like businesses. Some larger organizations have both an *executive director* and an *administrative director* who divide the administrative duties.

Requirements

Kennel attendants and adoption counselors usually need a high school diploma or GED certificate. Some shelters hire high school students who are legally of age to work and who show an aptitude for working with animals and with the public. High school classes in biology and other sciences help prepare students for working with shelter animals. English, speech, debate, and drama classes can help develop the self-confidence and verbal skills needed for interaction with the public and for interviewing adoption candidates. Mathematics, business, and computer courses build a foundation for the record-keeping and business-management aspects of these positions—and for promotions. (These high school course would also be of value to any employee in an animal shelter.) Most training is done on the job, and most promotions are made from within. Volunteering at a local shelter, kennel, or veterinary hospital is an excellent way to gain experience in this field while still in high school. Owning and caring for a pet and reading about animals, their care, and related topics can also be helpful.

Humane investigators would benefit from the same high school courses as kennel attendants and adoption counselors. In addition, many states require some college and special certification. College-level courses in law enforcement, psychology, animal science, animal behavior, and veterinary technology could be useful for humane investigators. Humane investigators must be nominated by a humane organization for the special training required for certification.

Humane educators are often teachers. Although there are presently no degree requirements for this position, shelters are beginning to look for humane educators who have degrees in education and related fields. In addition to the high school courses recommended for kennel workers, college or continuing education courses in psychology, public relations, and environmental education would be helpful to humane educators.

Shelter managers are frequently required to have a college degree, but experienced kennel workers who do not have degrees can be promoted into this position. Veterinary technicians or managers of other types of kennels might also be considered for a shelter manager position. An individual who hopes to become a shelter manager would be well advised to take college or continuing education courses in business management, veterinary technology, animal management, or animal husbandry.

Shelter administrators generally need a bachelor's degree or strong experience in business management or shelter management. Some executive director positions may even require a master's degree. Helpful areas of study include business administration and management, finance, public relations, fund-raising, grant writing, negotiations, and personnel development.

There are few, if any, internships and apprenticeships for animal shelter workers. Some veterinary medicine or veterinary technician programs do sponsor interns at animal shelters. A few colleges and universities offer individual courses for animal shelter directors or for humane educators, but those courses are difficult to find and are offered sporadically. The best educational opportunities are available through the national associations for animal welfare listed at the end of this chapter.

The position of humane investigator requires certification in some states. No other certification requirements exist for animal shelter workers at this time. No labor unions are associated with the field.

To make a good animal shelter worker, two of the most important ingredients are a respect for people and a love of animals. Animal shelter employees must work well with people in order to effectively promote the welfare of animals. They must be able to work independently and at the same time be good team players. They must be patient, compassionate, dedicated, organized, and hard working. Animal shelter workers need to be good communicators and good decision-makers. Rachel Hendricks started her animal welfare giving preliminary exams and doing lab work for the Community Animal Rescue Effort (CARE) at the Evanston Animal Shelter in Evanston, Illinois. She summed up the requirements for an animal shelter employee: "You have to work together. You have to love doing it. You get your rewards from the animals. It has to be in your heart."

Opportunities for Experience and Exploration

Public libraries have excellent books that give a detailed look into the world of animal shelters and humane societies. Many of the major national associations maintain Web sites that offer a variety of information and resources. Individuals who want to learn more about animal shelter work could contact a local shelter to inquire about humane education presentations that are scheduled in the community. They might attend humane education sessions or an open house at the shelter.

After some preliminary research, an individual might ask to interview a kennel worker or volunteer in order to learn about the position. Some shelters might agree to allow an interested person to spend a day following or working with a kennel worker.

Volunteering at a shelter is the best way to learn how you would like a career as an animal shelter employee. Animal shelters welcome volunteers who are considering a career as an animal shelter employee

Methods of Entering

The best way to get started in the field is to volunteer. Shelters depend heavily on volunteers, and loyal volunteers are first to be given an opportunity when a paid position opens. Most volunteers, like most animal shelter workers, start out as kennel workers and/or adoption counselors. The skills learned in those positions provide the basis for advancement. A helpful aspect of beginning a career as an animal shelter employee is that it is possible to enter the field from many backgrounds. A teacher might become a humane educator. A public health official could become a humane investigator. Business professionals and accountants could become shelter managers, administrators, or executive directors. It takes many skills to successfully run an animal shelter, and each individual can apply his or her expertise to improving the shelter and enhancing the welfare of the shelter animals.

Advancement

For animal shelter employees, most opportunities for advancement come from within. Since few formal training programs exist, on-the-job training provides the majority of learning and advancement opportunities. The national associations, such as AHA and the Humane Society of the United States (HSUS) publish training materials and sponsor training programs throughout the country. As animal shelter workers learn more and become more skilled, they are often promoted from one position to another. A good kennel attendant might be given the opportunity to study to become a humane investigator. An experienced kennel attendant, adoption counselor, humane investigator, or humane educator could eventually become a shelter manager. A shelter manager might become a shelter administrator. Any animal shelter employee who is interested in gaining a different position can study to acquire the skills needed for that position and work to acquire the experience.

In some cases, advancement may depend on the size of the shelter. Small shelters offer opportunities for employees to learn many skills, but they may not offer many avenues for advancement. Large shelters have more positions and more opportunities for advancement, but they may not provide the opportunity to learn as many skills at one time. Individuals may need to be willing to relocate to find a better chance for growth. Local animal shelters and newspaper listings are good places to look for local job openings. The national associations are good sources of information on job openings throughout the country.

Employment Outlook

According to the Humane Society of the United States and the American Humane Association, the United States is in a pet-overpopulation crisis. A 1996 survey conducted by the American Pet Products Manufacturers Association found that there were about 66.2 million cats and 58 million dogs in this country. Despite early spay/neuter programs and the concerted efforts of shelters and veterinarians to reduce the problem, the overpopulation is expected to continue into the twenty-first century. According to the 1997-1998 edition of the *Occupational Outlook Handbook*, although the pet population may eventually decline, the demand for animal shelter workers will probably remain steady. Turnover is often high among kennel workers due to the strenuous physical work and generally low income level. As a result, the availability of jobs should be good for those workers.

At middle-management and upper-management levels, Doug Trowbridge of AHA predicts that jobs will keep pace with those of entry-level positions due to the increasing number of shelters and types of positions within them. According to HSUS's Pet Population Fact Sheet, there are between four and six thousand animal shelters in the United States.

John Walsh, International Projects Director of the World Society for the Protection of Animals Boston office, states that there is increasing awareness of the plight of domestic animals and wildlife throughout the world. He projects that the outlook should be very good for the future for those interested in animal shelter and welfare work at the international level.

Earnings

There is a wide range of salaries and benefits for animal shelter employees. Some differences depend on the size and location of the shelter. Large shelters in metropolitan areas generally offer higher pay and more benefits. Small shelters and those in rural areas may offer lower salaries, and some may only provide part-time employment.

Nicholas Gilman, the Director of Field Services for the American Humane Association, states that salaries for middle managers range from $10,000 to $40,000 or $50,000. According to Mr. Gilman, senior manager salaries can range from $20,000 to $100,000, while executive directors earn between $20,000 and $150,000.

Other salary differences depend on the duties of the shelter employee. Entry-level kennel workers and adoption counselors often start at minimum wage. They earn around $9,500 a year if they work full time. With experience and training, salaries for these positions increase. A salary survey published by the National Animal Control Association showed that in 1996, nonsupervisory animal caretakers who worked in animal care agencies earned an average of about $17,100 per year.

Most shelters offer at least a health insurance benefit, though some may not. Some health insurance plans require that the employee contribute a part of the monthly premium. Shelters offer retirement plans. Some of the larger shelters and associations have very attractive benefit packages.

Conditions of Work

Animal shelter employees have the moral satisfaction of promoting the welfare of animals. They feel joy and pride because they make a difference in the lives of animals and people. They may also experience sadness and anger at the suffering they witness among the animals that are sick, injured, or abused. In some shelters, suffering or unadoptable animals are euthanized. Animal shelter employees may be upset when this is necessary. Individuals who are philosophically or emotionally opposed to euthanasia can choose to work in no-kill shelters where the animals are kept until they are adopted.

For most animal shelter employees, schedules and hours of work vary. In smaller shelters, and even in some larger ones, everyone—including the executive director—may be involved in the care and feeding of the animals. If the work is not done at the end of an eight hour day, it must be completed. Most shelters are staffed twenty-four hours a day every day of the year. Weekend, evening, and holiday work is often required.

Shelter kennel attendants have the pleasure of working closely with the animals. This can be enjoyable and satisfying. Kennel workers wear comfortable, casual clothes, which many employees consider a benefit. Most of the work is inside the shelter, but animals are sometimes exercised outside. Keeping animals and their habitats clean is physically demanding. Kennel workers lift and move heavy animals, cages, and bags of feed. They also have to bend and stoop to work with animals and clean cages. Kennels are often noisy and sometimes have strong or unpleasant odors. Workers may be exposed to hazardous chemicals in cleaning agents. They may be bitten, scratched, or kicked by animals. Some workers may be allergic to animals. The work can be repetitive, but the animals themselves provide variety.

Adoption counselors also work closely with the animals. They get to know the personalities of the animals so they can try to match each animal with an appropriate home. Counselors work mostly indoors. They work in the kennel area and in the office. Many shelters provide private rooms where the counselors meet with adoption applicants. Depending on the philosophy of the shelter and their other duties, adoption counselors may dress casually or in office attire. Since they work with the public, adoption counselors may experience stress when dealing with unpleasant, angry, or unreasonable people.

Humane investigators work indoors and outdoors. Their clothing may be casual, or they may wear uniforms. Their duties are physically demanding. They have to run, climb, crawl, or swim to catch strays or rescue trapped or injured animals. They may be hurt by animals that feel threatened. They may also be exposed to rabies and other communicable diseases carried by the animals they rescue. Confronting individuals accused of animal neglect or abuse can be stressful and even dangerous. Humane investigators may be on call for emergencies; weekend and evening work is likely.

Humane educators usually work indoors. They dress in casual or office attire, depending on their schedule and other duties. They frequently travel around the community. Humane educators from larger shelters may travel around the state or country. Their work involves the stress of working with the public, and they frequently have deadlines for developing materials and presentations.

Shelter managers work indoors and outdoors. They work in an office and in the shelter kennels. Their attire can vary depending on the philosophy of the shelter and the work they are performing on a given day. They may be exposed to hazardous chemicals. They may experience stress due to supervising volunteers and employees and dealing with the public.

Shelter administrators work mostly indoors in quiet offices. Most dress in professional attire, but those who also work in the kennels may dress more casually. Administrators travel to community events and meetings, and they may travel for fund-raising purposes. They can experience a high degree of stress related to financial matters, business management, and public relations.

Sources of Additional Information

The American Humane Association (AHA) works to protect both children and animals. It is an excellent source of low-cost information on many animal welfare topics. Its Web site lists current job opportunities in animal protection, including requirements and some salaries. The Web site also has links to other animal welfare organizations.

The American Humane Association
63 Inverness Drive East
Englewood, CO 80112
Tel: 303-792-9900
Email: APinfo@americanhumane.org
WWW: http://www.americanhumane.org

The American Society for the Prevention of Cruelty to Animals (ASPCA) has an outreach department that offers free and low-cost information on animal welfare and pet care topics. The ASPCA provides training programs for shelter workers. Its Web site details its services and provides links to other humane organizations' Web sites.

The American Society for the Prevention of Cruelty to Animals
424 East 92nd Street
New York, NY 10128-6804
Tel: 212-876-7700
WWW: http://www.aspca.org

The Humane Society of the United States (HSUS) advocates for animals, the earth, and the environment. Its Web site has educational articles, details the organization's goals, and provides links to other humane organizations.

The Humane Society of the United States
2100 L Street, NW
Washington, DC 20037
Tel: 202-452-1100
Email: webmaster@hsus.org
WWW: http://www.hsus.org

The World Society for the Protection of Animals (WSPA) is an international agency that provides relief to animals throughout the world. It is made up of more than three hundred humane societies from seventy-two countries. Its primary focus is developing animal protective programs at the government level. WSPA serves as the international "Red Cross" for animals in need anywhere in the world.

The World Society for the Protection of Animals
PO Box 190
Boston, MA 02130
Tel: 617-522-7000
WWW: http://way.net/wspa

The World Society for the Protection of Animals
2 Langley Lane
London SW8 1TJ
England
Email: wspa@wspa.org.uk

Animal Trainers

School Subjects

Anatomy and Physiology
Biology
Psychology

Personal Interests

Entertaining/Performing
Helping people: personal service
Helping people: physical health
Helping people: protection
Wildlife

Work Environment

Indoors and outdoors
One location with some travel

Minimum Education Level

Some postsecondary training

Salary Range

$10,000 to $25,000 to $50,000

Certification or Licensing

Required by certain specialties:
racehorse trainers

Outlook

Decline

Definition

Animal trainers teach animals to obey commands so the animals can be counted on to perform these tasks in given situations. The animals can be trained for up to several hundred commands, to compete in shows or races, to perform tricks to entertain audiences, to protect property, or act as guides for the disabled. Animal trainers may work with several types of animals or specialize with one type.

History

Animals have been used for their skills for hundreds of years. The St. Bernard has assisted in search and rescue missions in the Swiss Alps for more than three hundred years. The German shepherd was used in Germany after the First World War to guide blind veterans.

Dorothy Eustis, after visiting the program in Germany, founded the first American program for training guide dogs, called the Seeing Eye, in 1929. Basing the training program on the one that she visited in Potsdam, Eustis's program launched others that were modeled or developed from hers. The Seeing Eye still has only one facility in the United States, in Morristown, New Jersey, but dozens of programs now exist for the training of guide dogs for the blind.

Other programs began to utilize the guide dog training system to provide animal-based assistance to other disabled individuals. Most of these programs are less than twenty years old, and the majority of the programs were developed in the late 1980s and the 1990s. Programs now exist for a variety of animals over a range of disabilities for which an animal can be of assistance.

Programs to train search-and-rescue dogs in the United States are new, particularly compared to the programs in Europe. The Swiss program inspired search-and-rescue dog training programs in the United States in the 1970s. Various small programs were developed that relied on individuals with specific breeds of dogs to volunteer to train their pets for disaster or search operations. Programs such as the Black Paws for the Newfoundland breed offer certification that is accepted by law enforcement and search teams in selecting animals for search operations. After receiving state-recognized certification, dog and handler teams can choose to continue training for more intensive programs.

The Federal Emergency Management Agency (FEMA) established criteria and certification testing for disaster search dog and handler teams in 1991. They started with a few teams, funding established dog and dog-handler teams to undergo an intensive training program. In 1995, when the bombing of the Murrah Federal Building in Oklahoma occurred, twenty American teams were FEMA certified. The FEMA goal was revised after the bombing, to have three hundred teams certified at all times for emergency situations; however, in 1998, only twenty-five teams were certified and there were no plans to increase team funding.

Nature of the Work

Many animals are capable of being trained. The techniques used to train them are basically the same, regardless of the type of animal. Animal trainers conduct programs consisting primarily of repetition and reward to teach animals to behave in a particular manner and to do it consistently.

First, trainers evaluate an animal's temperament, ability, and aptitude to determine its trainability. Animals vary in personality, just as people do. Some animals are more stubborn, willful, or easily distracted, and would not do well with rigid training programs. All animals can be trained at some level, but certain animals are more receptive to training; these animals are chosen for programs that demand great skill.

One of the most familiar examples is the seeing-eye dog, now usually called a companion animal for the blind. These dogs are trained with several hundred verbal commands to assist their human and to recognize potentially dangerous situations. The dog must be able to, without any command, walk his companion around obstacles on the sidewalk. The companion dog must be able to read street lights and know to cross at the green, and only after traffic has cleared. The dog must also not be tempted to run to greet other dogs, grab food, or behave as most pet dogs do. Very few dogs make it through the rigorous training program. The successful dogs have proved to be such aids to the visually impaired that similar programs have been developed to train dogs for people who are confined to a wheelchair, or are hearing impaired, or incapable of executing some aspect of a day-to-day routine where a dog can assist.

By painstakingly repeating routines many times and rewarding the animal when it does what is expected, animal trainers train an animal to obey or perform on command or, in certain situations, without command. In addition, animal trainers are responsible for the feeding, exercising, grooming, and general care of the animals, either handling the duties themselves or supervising other workers. In some training programs, trainers come in and work with the animals; in other programs, such as the companion animal program, the animal lives with the trainer for the duration of the program.

Trainers usually specialize in one type of animal and are identified by this type of animal. *Dog trainers*, for example, may work with police dogs, training them to search for drugs or missing people. The programs to train drug-detecting dogs use different detection responses, but each dog is trained in only one response system. Some dogs are trained to behave passively when the scent is detected, with a quiet signal given to the accompanying police officer that drugs have been detected. The signal can be sitting next to the scent, pointing, or following. Other dogs are trained to dig, tear, and destroy containers that have the drug in them. As one animal trainer from the U.S. Customs office pointed out, these dogs may be a nightmare pet because they can destroy a couch in seconds, but they make great drug-detecting dogs. The common breeds for companion dogs and police dogs are German shepherds, rottweilers, and Labrador retrievers.

Some train guard dogs to protect private property; others train dogs for performance, where the dog may learn numerous stunts or movements with hand commands so that the dog can perform on a stage or in film without the audience hearing the commands spoken from offstage. Shepherding dogs are also trained with whistle or hand commands because commands may have to be given from some distance away from where the dog is working.

Dogs, partly because of the variety of breeds available and partly because of their nature to work for approval, have countless roles for which they are trained. Even pet dogs may be trained by animal trainers who work with owners to teach the dog routine commands that make walking the dog safer and easier, or break the dog of destructive or dangerous habits.

Horse trainers specialize in training horses for riding or for harness. They talk to and handle a horse gently to accustom it to human contact, then gradually get it to accept a harness, bridle, saddle, and other riding gear. Trainers teach horses to respond to commands that are either spoken or given by use of the reins and legs. Draft horses are conditioned to draw equipment either alone or as part of a team. Show horses are given special training to qualify them to perform in competitions. Horse trainers sometimes have to retrain animals that have developed bad habits, such as bucking or biting. Besides feeding, exercising, and grooming, these trainers may make arrangements for breeding the horses and help mares deliver their foals.

A highly specialized occupation in the horse-training field is that of *racehorse trainers*, who must create individualized training plans for every horse in their care. By studying the animal's performance record and becoming familiar with its behavior during workouts, trainers can adapt their training methods to take advantage of each animal's peculiarities. Like other animal trainers, racehorse trainers oversee the exercising, grooming, and feeding of their charges. They also clock the running time during workouts to determine when a horse is ready for competitive racing. Racehorse trainers coach jockeys on how best to handle a particular horse during a race and may give owners advice on purchasing horses.

Police horse trainers work with police horses to keep them from startling in crowds or responding to other animals in their presence. As with the police dogs, these animals require a very stable, calm personality that remains no matter what the situation the animal works in. Police officers who work with animals on a routine basis develop strong attachments to the animals.

Other animal trainers work with more exotic animals for performance or for health reasons. The dolphins and whales at the Shedd Aquarium in Chicago are trained to roll over, lift fins and tails, and open their mouths on command, so that much veterinary work can be done without anesthesia, which is always dangerous for animals. These skills are demonstrated for the public every day, so they function as a show for people, but the overriding reason for training the dolphins is to keep them healthy. Other training elements include teaching dolphins to retrieve items from the bottom of their pool, so that if any visitor throws or loses something in the pool, divers are not required to invade the dolphins' space.

Animal trainers work with hunting birds, training them to fly after an injury, or to hunt if the bird was found as a hatchling before a parent had trained it. Birds that are successfully trained to fly and hunt can be released into the wild; the others may remain in educational programs where they will perform for audiences. It is, however, illegal to keep any releasable hunting bird for more than one year in the United States.

Each species of animal is trained by using the instincts and reward systems that are appropriate to that species. Hunting birds are rewarded with food; they don't enjoy petting and do not respond warmly to human touch, unless they were hand-raised from hatching by humans. Dogs, on the other hand, respond immediately to petting and gentle handling, unless they were handled inappropriately or viciously by someone. Sea mammals respond to both food and physical contact.

Some animal species are generally difficult to train. Sea otters are extremely destructive naturally and do not train easily. African elephants are much more difficult to train than Asian elephants, and females are much more predictable and trainable than the larger males. Most circus elephants are Asian because they are much easier to handle. Captive elephants, though, kill more handlers and keepers than every other species combined.

Requirements

For high school students interested in becoming an animal trainer, courses in anatomy and physiology, biology, and psychology may be helpful. Understanding how the body works helps a trainer understand what an animal can do. Psychology may help the trainer recognize behaviors in the animals they train, as well as in the people they are training the animals for.

Although there are no formal education requirements to enter this field, some positions do have educational requirements that include a college degree. Animal trainers in circuses and the entertainment field may be required to have some education in animal psychology in addition to their caretaking experience. Zoo and aquarium animal trainers usually must have a B.S. or B.A. in a field related to animal management or animal physiology. Trainers of companion dogs prepare for their work in a three-year course of study at schools that train dogs and instruct the disabled owner-companion.

Most trainers begin their careers as keepers and gain on-the-job experience in evaluating the disposition, intelligence, and "trainability" of the animals they look after. At the same time, they learn to make friends with their charges, develop a rapport with them, and gain their confidence. The caretaking experience is an important building block in the education and success of an animal trainer. Although previous training experience may give job applicants an advantage in being hired, they still will be expected to spend time caring for the animals before advancing to a trainer position.

Prospective animal trainers should like and respect animals and have a genuine interest in working with them. With most of the career options for an animal trainer, there is an underlying desire to help people as well. Most trained animals work with people to accomplish a goal, so the relationship between the animal, the trainer, and the owner or companion is an important one. It requires the trainer to be thoughtful, sensitive, and well-spoken. Also, the trainer should be prepared to work intensely with an animal and then have that animal go on to work somewhere else. The relationship with the trained animal may not be permanent, so separation is part of the trainer's job.

Establishments that hire trainers often require previous animal-keeping or equestrian experience as proper care and feeding of animals is an essential part of a trainer's responsibilities. These positions serve as informal apprenticeships. The assistant may get to help an animal trainer on certain tasks, but will be able to watch and learn from other tasks being performed around him or her. For example, racehorse trainers often begin as jockeys or grooms in training stables.

Racehorse trainers must be licensed by the state in which they work. Otherwise, there are no special requirements for this occupation.

Opportunities for Experience and Exploration

Students wishing to enter this field would do well to learn as much as they can about animals, especially animal psychology, either through coursework or library study. Interviews with animal trainers and tours of their workplaces might be arranged to provide firsthand information about the practical aspects of this occupation.

Volunteering offers an opportunity to begin training with animals and learning first-hand about the tasks and routines involved in managing animals, as well as training them. Part-time or volunteer work in animal shelters, pet-training programs, rescue centers, pet shops, or veterinary offices gives potential trainers a chance to discover whether they have the aptitude for working with animals. Experience can be acquired, too, in summer jobs as animal caretakers at zoos, aquariums, museums that feature live animal shows, amusement parks, and for those with a special interest in horse racing, at stables.

Methods of Entering

People who wish to become animal trainers generally start out as animal keepers, stable workers, or caretakers and rise to the position of trainer only after acquiring experience within the ranks of an organization. You can enter the field by applying directly for a job as animal keeper, letting your employer or supervisor know of your ambition so you will eventually be considered for promotion. The same applies for volunteer positions. Learning as a volunteer is an excellent way to get hands-on experience, but you should be vocal in your interest in a paid position once you have gotten to know the staff and they have gotten to know you.

You should pay close attention to the training methods of any place you are considering working. No reputable organization, regardless of what it trains animals for, should use physical injury to train or discipline an animal. The techniques you learn at your first job determine the position you will qualify for after that. You want to be sure that you are witnessing and learning from an organization that has a sound philosophy and training method for working with animals.

The most coveted positions depend on the animals you want to work with. Sea mammals are a specialty of oceanariums and aquariums, and these positions are fiercely competitive. Dog-training programs are probably the most plentiful, and offer the widest range of training philosophies and techniques. There are numerous books on dog training methods that you should consult to know what the differences are.

FEMA only works with established dog and handler teams, who usually work within the emergency systems for the regional or local authorities in some capacity. These teams choose to also be trained within the FEMA guidelines.

Advancement

Most establishments have very small staffs of animal trainers, which means that the opportunities for advancement are limited. The progression is from animal keeper to animal trainer. A trainer who directs or supervises others may be designated *head animal trainer* or *senior animal trainer*.

Some animal trainers go into business for themselves and, if successful, hire other trainers to work for them. Others become *agents* for animal acts. But promotion may mean moving from one organization to another, and may require relocating to another city, depending on what animal you specialize in.

Employment Outlook

The demand for animal trainers is not great as most employers have little need for a large staff and tend to promote from within. This field is expected to decline through the year 2006. Criticism of animals used for purely entertainment purposes has reduced the number used for shows and performances. But as programs expand for companion animals and animals used in work settings, the opportunity in those fields may increase slightly. In all fields, applicants must be well qualified to overcome the heavy competition for available jobs. Some openings may be created as zoos and aquariums expand or provide more animal shows in an effort to increase revenue. Search-and-rescue programs, although expanding, are not permanent work positions for the handler. These teams are used intermittently, as the need arises. But a slightly increased number of trainers will be needed to train the increased number of teams.

Earnings

Salaries of animal trainers can vary widely according to specialty and place of employment. Salaries can range from $10,000 to $100,000 a year, depending on the type of training done. However, animal training jobs are generally low-paying, with average rates between minimum wage and $10 an hour, even for the self-employed. A few of the specialists, such as those working with dolphins in aquariums, can earn in the mid-$20,000s, but very few individuals earn much more. Those who do earn the higher salaries are in upper management and spend more time running the business than working with animals.

In the field of racehorse training, however, trainers are paid an average fee of $35 to $50 a day for each horse, plus 10 percent of any money their horses win in races. Depending on the horse and the races it runs, this can exceed the average high-end earnings for a trainer. Show horse trainers may earn as much as $30,000 to $35,000 a year. Trainers in business for themselves set their own fees for teaching both horses and owners.

Conditions of Work

The working hours for animal trainers vary considerably, depending on the type of animal, performance schedule, and whether travel is involved. For some trainers, such as those who work with show horses, educational programs with hunting birds, or new animals being brought into zoos and aquariums, the hours can be long and quite irregular. Travel is common, and will probably include responsibility for seeing to the animals' needs while on the road. This can include feeding, creative housing, and driving with the animal. For one program director of a rescue center that works with injured hawks, it means traveling frequently for educational shows with a suitcase full of frozen rats and chicks for food.

Much of the work is conducted outdoors. In winter, trainers may work indoors, but depending on the animal, they may continue outdoor training year round. If the animal is expected to work or perform outdoors in winter, they have to be trained in winter as well. Companion animals have to cope with every type of weather, so the trainer is responsible for training and testing the animal accordingly.

Working with certain animals requires physical strength; for example, it takes arm strength to hold a falcon on your wrist for an hour, or to control an eighty-pound dog who doesn't want to heel. Other aspects of the work may require lifting, bending, or extended periods of standing or swimming. Trainers of aquatic mammals, such as dolphins and seals, work in water and must feel comfortable in aquatic environments.

Patience is essential to the job as well. Just as people do, animals have bad days where they won't work well and respond to commands. So even the best trainer encounters days of frustration where nothing seems to go well. Trainers must spend long hours repeating routines and rewarding their pupils for performing well, while never getting angry with them or punishing them when they fail to do what is expected. Trainers must be able to exhibit the authority to keep animals under control without raising their voices or using physical force. Calmness under stress is particularly important when dealing with wild animals.

Sources of Additional Information

American Zoo and Aquarium Association
7970-D Old Georgetown Road
Bethesda, MD 20814-2493
Tel: 301-907-7777
WWW: http://www.aza.org/

The AquaThought Foundation is a privately funded research organization dedicated to the exploration of human-dolphin interaction.

AquaThought Foundation
15951 McGregor Boulevard, Suite 2C
Fort Myers, FL 33908
Tel: 941-437-2958WWW: http://www.aquathought.com

Canadian Association of Zoological Parks and Aquariums
Calgary Zoo
PO Box 3036
Calgary, AB T2M 4R8 Canada
Tel: 403-232-9300

Canine Companions for Independence
National Headquarters
PO Box 446
Santa Rosa, CA 95402-0446
Tel: 800-572-2275 (also TDD)

The Delta Society currently provides certification programs in animal evaluation and in training animal handlers for animal-assisted therapy and companion animal training.

Delta Society
289 Perimeter Road East
Renton, WA 98055-1329
Tel: 800-869-6898
WWW: http://www2.deltasociety.org

Dogs for the Deaf, Inc., rescues and professionally trains dogs to assist hearing-impaired people.

Dogs for the Deaf, Inc.
10175 Wheeler Road
Central Point, OR 97502
Tel: 541-826-9220 (also TDD)
Email: info@dogsforthedeaf.org
WWW: http://www.dogsforthedeaf.org

The Humane Society of the United States
Animal Caretakers Information
Companion Animals Division
2100 L Street, NW
Washington, DC 20037
Tel: 202-452-1100
WWW: htpp://www.hsus.org

National Disaster Search Dog Foundation
323 East Matilija Avenue #110-245
Ojai, CA 93023-2740
Tel: 805-639-3840
Email: rescue@west.net

Equestrian Management Workers

Definition

Equestrian management includes a wide variety of positions such as *farriers, horse breeders, horse trainers, judges, jockeys, stable managers, riding instructors, farm managers, racetrack managers, equine insurance adjusters, breed association managers, race association managers*, and related business, sales, and marketing positions.

History

Historically valued for work and transportation, horses have been in use since 2000 BC when they were domesticated in Babylonia. Evidence indicates that they were in use in Egypt three hundred years later. Chariots with mounted soldiers were popular in parades, and equestrian displays were featured in early Olympic Games in Greece and at ancient Roman celebrations. By the fourteenth century, horses were in general use by knights, with a fast, light horse (a palfrey) used for travel, and a sturdier war-horse (like a quarterhorse) used to carry the knight in battle. Because of the extreme weight of the knight's and the horse's armor, the horses had to be durable, stocky animals.

Pages were young boys, usually born to noble families, who learned under the tutelage of knights and squires how to care for and ride horses, and acquire the other skills they would be expected to know. As they improved and got older, they would serve as a knight's squire, learning the skills for battle, and assisting the knight in actual battles. Squires worked with the knight's horses and led the war-horse as the knight rode the palfrey. He then kept the palfrey safe while the knight fought or jousted. Eventually a squire might become a knight himself.

The swiftest transportation across land for the next five hundred years was by horse. Horses were either ridden or used to pull carriages or other transport. The fastest traveler could go fifty miles a day; the average traveler on horseback made about half that distance. Roads were unreliable, unpassable in winter or rainy weather, and travelers had to find places to stay that could accommodate horses as well. The expense of buying and keeping a horse, or a team of horses for some carriages, restricted their use to well-to-do and wealthy families. Mules were more common for transporting goods, and walking was frequently how people traveled, even for journeys of hundreds or thousands of miles. Travelers on foot could go eight to twelve miles a day on average, so it took at least twice as long on foot as it did by horse to travel anywhere.

In the sixteenth century, Spanish conquistadors brought the first horses to America. The horse population increased as horses were left to breed in wild packs. Eventually Native American tribes incorporated horses into their lifestyle, by capturing and domesticating the animals. European settlers also were familiar with horses for both transportation and farming purposes, so they too brought and used horses.

Interest in horses changed from functional to recreational in the late 1800s and early 1900s. Trains replaced horse travel as the fastest transportation across land. Trains were not only faster, they were more reliable and safer for travelers. Gasoline and diesel-powered vehicles such as the car and the tractor replaced the horse for both local travel and farming needs. By the 1930s, in all but the least developed countries, the horse became an animal for leisure activities only. Horses are used now for Western and English riding, rodeos, and horse racing, and rarely for other activities. Stable owners and landowners hire the workers who care for the horses used in these activities.

Nature of the Work

Horses are owned, ridden, raced, and shown in every state in the nation. With nearly seven million domesticated horses in the United States alone, the staff needed to care for and train these animals is immense. From riding trainers to the people who manage stables with dozens of animals, the range of jobs and the range of places to work is large.

Equestrian management positions include "contact" and "noncontact" positions. Contact jobs are hands-on positions actually working with horses, at a track, on a farm, or with a breeding association. Noncontact jobs may involve working in the marketing department of a race track, breeder, riding stable, or as a salesperson for equipment, feed, insurance, or equine pharmaceuticals.

Equine-related careers require long hours, whether a person is working directly with horses or in an office setting. Regardless of the position, employers look for people with a knowledge of horses, flexibility, and a willingness to start small and work their way up. For example, a riding instructor may work from 6:00 AM to 10:00 PM if a schedule mandates such lesson times. There may be long breaks, but during show season, days can be long. An instructor may take two or twenty pupils to a horse show and be responsible for coaching them before, during, and after classes. Riding instructors may work with students who are looking to enter a riding competition or who are just riding for pleasure. Students range from youngsters to retired people looking to develop a new hobby.

Training can be for dressage, which involves riding a horse through a series of complex maneuvers to demonstrate agility and responsiveness of the horse and control of the rider. Jumping is riding the horse through a varied obstacle course. Combined training, or eventing, is the triathlon of equestrian sports, incorporating dressage, cross-country jumping, and show jumping. Riders compete at all levels of competition, including Olympic levels. Trainers usually specialize, unless they train for eventing.

A stable manager is similar to a store manager. Responsibilities include ensuring feed and bedding are well stocked and ordered, as well as medicating and monitoring sick or injured horses. The duties of stable managers include hiring personnel to clean stalls and feed, exercise, and groom horses. In a small operation, the manager may do such tasks. He or she may organize clinics or shows at a stable for large groups of riders, and work with judges, stewards, food vendors, and various horse organizations. Turning a horse out to a paddock or pasture daily is usually necessary for a horse's health. In a large stable, a manager must know the personality, temperament, and physical needs of each horse. The types of things the manager notes about each horse can be which horses get along with certain riders or other horses, which ones must be left alone in a paddock, which have physical ailments, and such details as when the horse was last ridden, groomed, inspected, fed, watered, and checked by the vet. New horses have to be introduced to the herd by a process of increasing interaction spent with a new horse and its pasture mates.

Jockeys ride racehorses. A *harness driver* sits in a sulky and guides trotters around the track; a *steeplechase jockey* rides a horse cross-country on a course with large brush jumps; and a *flat racing jockey* rides horses on a flat track at varying distances. Many jockeys work as freelancers, riding for different barns, trainers, and owners. A good jockey may be hired by a specific barn for a whole season because of a particularly good relationship with a certain horse. Generally, jockeys have fairly stable working hours during racing season but usually begin early in the morning and finish in early evening after a day of racing.

Judges are used at all levels and disciplines with the horse industry. Horse showing is popular from the 4-H club level to the international show circuit. Judges grade and place riders in order of excellence. Some judges travel internationally, and others may officiate each summer at a local show.

Veterinary technicians are the equivalent of nurses in the veterinary field. They tend to general animal care and do tests, administer medicine, perform radiology exams or ultrasound therapy, and provide wound care.

Farriers, a word that comes from the medieval French word for iron (ferrour), refers to people who shoe horses and care for their hooves and feet. Horses' hooves grow the way fingernails do, so they require trimming and grooming, and, to protect the hoof, a farrier may put an iron ring on the bottom of the hoof. These are the semicircle items called horseshoes. A farrier may have to make horseshoes, but he or she is always required to customize the shoe for each horse, even if the iron rings are not made by hand.

The equine industry is a business like any other, so capable administrators with a knowledge of horses and office management are necessary. One administrative position is that of an *equine marketing representative* whose duties include promoting and organizing horse shows and races. Marketing representatives also develop brochures and video tapes of horses and their offspring to promote various breed associations. They may work in insurance, providing life insurance coverage for valuable horses which are used for breeding, performing, or racing.

Requirements

For information on requirements specific to the careers of animal breeders and technicians, and veterinary technicians, see those chapters.

High school students should take biology courses. If your school has any riding classes, clubs, or teams, you should consider participating. Any experience around horses is helpful and gives you an item for your resume.

Instructing requires patience and the ability to calm nervous students. Many universities offer certification for riding instruction at beginning, intermediate, and advanced levels. Riding instructors or trainers must have an extensive background in riding or teaching and possibly certification from an accredited school.

College courses can include anatomy, animal physiology, health, and business management. Each will give you some flexibility in job training.

Stable management positions may also require a degree from an accredited two-year program. Students learn everything from feeding rations and veterinary maintenance to handling troublesome horses and managing a show. Long hours may be required depending upon how busy the stable is with lessons and how many horses are in the facility.

Being a farrier requires great physical strength, especially in the arms and back. Certification is required from an accredited school (usually a six-week full-time course), and an apprenticeship with an experienced farrier is highly recommended. It is not absolutely necessary to have a background with horses; however, a good and respected farrier will have an excellent eye in spotting problems with a horse's gait and the ability to know what is wrong with its movements just from watching. To become a trainer, a person must know how to groom and care for horses and build a reputation as a competent trainer who is sensitive to a horse's needs and abilities.

Being a judge requires good horsemanship, a good eye, and several years' experience in the horse industry. Depending on the show and riding discipline, some judges may need accreditation or training experience or must attend certain courses and clinics.

For dressage competitions, certification may be required. The U.S. Dressage Federation (USDF) certifies for both participants and trainers in dressage competition. Active participants in the following programs will need to be USDF participating members: pre-certification clinic participants (excluding auditors); instructor certification testing candidates; certification examiners; certified instructors; USDF judges' seminar participants (excluding those seminars specifically required to maintain an American Horse Show Association judge license); judge session and testing participants (excluding auditors); and judge program faculty.

Computer skills are increasingly important in this field. Anyone expecting to advance through management ranks should have a college degree. Some colleges and universities offer equine management or science programs, and students often take business administration courses.

A college degree is not mandatory for sales positions, but it is preferable. More importantly, knowledge of the horse industry and enthusiasm is required to be a successful sales representative.

Opportunities for Experience and Exploration

Visiting a local stable, taking riding lessons, and joining 4-H are the easiest ways to begin to explore the career possibilities in equestrian management. Any experience with horses will only help your career. Access to most of the jobs described here can be gained by starting at the bottom and working with and around horses. A part-time job at a stable or grooming horses for a trainer will net valuable experience for the potential jockey, trainer, or salesperson.

Methods of Entering

Aside from administrators and managers, anyone interested in a career with horses should take riding lessons. Some stables need part-time and full-time help depending on the season and location. Many larger facilities offer positions where a person may clean stalls, feed and groom horses, and maintain stables. It is possible to negotiate an exchange of services for riding lessons, where you can gain experience both as a rider as well as a groom, in a volunteer position.

Although all states have stables and riding schools, Kentucky is the heart of the horse industry, with many other southern states dominating the market with their internationally acclaimed breeders and stables.   Texas and

California also have a large percentage of the horse populations in every category, from racing horses to work horses.

Advancement

It is possible to go from lower level grooming jobs to higher level positions. A farrier or veterinary technician may become self-employed after building a reputation and customer base.

With proper certification and a four-year college degree, it's possible to start work in entry-level management and progress. Top management positions require a business degree.

Employment Outlook

The horse industry was on the decline in the late 1980s. A recession, revised tax laws, and competition with other sports and forms of gambling took dollars away from the industry that had been on a steady incline since the 1960s. Although it has stabilized in the 1990s, not many farms are being sold.

There is an oversupply of farm managers since many farms have gone out of business, but opportunities for farriers and veterinarian technicians are plentiful. A lot of farm work is seasonal, and most people who work with horses have another form of income they use to support their horse business.

Earnings

Entry-level stable management workers earn minimum wage. Sometimes they get free housing on the farm where they work. The yearly earnings of stable managers and other administrators vary depending on the size and success of the farm, but in general are somewhere between $20,000 and $60,000. Horse breeders may earn from $19,000 to $50,000 a year. Horse trainers earn from $15,000 to $45,000 a year depending on years of experience, reputation, commissions on horses they have sold, and on the breeds. If a trainer can rent out all of his stalls, instead of putting his own horses in them, he can earn more money to pay for expenses. Most judges have other jobs and get paid for each show they judge. Their pay ranges from $300 to $500 per show. Farriers may earn $18,000 a year to start, and their earning ceiling is about $30,000 a year. Veterinary technicians earn between $14,000 and $27,000 a year. Marketing representatives start at $18,000 in entry-level positions, but over several years their earning potential is unlimited. Sales representatives start low at $14,000 a year, but usually also receive a bonus or commission. Their income potential, like the marketing representative, is limited only by the market and their own drive.

Conditions of Work

Most positions in the horse industry require long hours, especially during show season. Many contract, or farm, positions are seasonal, requiring employees to have some other form of employment to support their equine career. Persons interested in these careers should enjoy working with horses in the entire spectrum of conditions.

Sources of Additional Information

American Horse Council
1700 K Street, NW
Washington, DC 20006
Tel: 202-296-4031

American Horse Show Association
220 East 42nd Street
New York, NY 10017-5876
Tel: 212-972-2472

American Riding Instructors Association
PO Box 282
Alton Bay, NH 03810-0282
Tel: 603-875-4000
Email: aricp@aria.win.net
WWW: http://www.win.net/aria/aria.html

American Youth Horse Council
4193 Iron Works Pike
Lexington, KY 40511-2742

Thoroughbred Owners and Breeders Association
PO Box 4367
Lexington, KY 40544
Tel: 606-276-2291
Email: toba@iglou.com
WWW: http://www.toba.org

United States Combined Training Association, Inc.
525 Old Waterford Road, NW
Leesburg, VA 20176
Tel: 703-779-0440
WWW: http://www.eventingusa.com

Naturalists

Biology Earth science	School Subjects
The Environment Plants/gardening	Personal Interests
Primarily outdoors Primarily one location	Work Environment
Bachelor's degree	Minimum Education Level
$15,000 to $25,000 to $70,000	Salary Range
None	Certification or Licensing
About as fast as the average	Outlook
049	DOT
11.07.03	GOE
2121	NOC

Definition

The primary role of *naturalists* is to educate the public about the environment and maintain the natural environment on land specifically dedicated to wilderness populations. Naturalists are usually given a specific title, according to their job tasks, but their primary responsibility is always related to preserving, restoring, maintaining, and protecting a natural or seminatural habitat. Among the related responsibilities in these jobs are teaching, public speaking, writing, giving scientific and ecological demonstrations, and handling public relations and administrative tasks. Naturalists work in private nature centers; local, state, and national parks and forests; wildlife museums; and independent nonprofit conservation and restoration associations.

Among the many job titles a naturalist might hold are *wildlife manager, fish and game warden, fish and wildlife officer, land steward, wildlife biologist,* and *environmental interpreter. Natural resources managers, wildlife conservationists,* and *ecologists* sometimes perform the work of a naturalist.

History

The ancient Greeks named and observed the properties of plants and animals. Aristotle, Theophrastus, and other Greek philosophers investigated the properties of flora and fauna alike. In the Roman Empire, the scholar Pliny wrote treatises on natural history. Among the earliest naturalists may have been those in occupations essentially connected to nature, such as gardeners, shepherds, vine-growers, hunters, and fishers, as well as those who studied and used plants for their medicinal value.

Despite the interest in nature, there was little support for environmental preservation before the seventeenth century. Instead, wilderness was commonly seen as a vast resource to be controlled. This view began to change during the early years of the Industrial Revolution, when new energy resources were utilized, establishing an increasing need for petroleum, coal, natural gas, wood, and water for hydropowered energy. In England and France, for example, the rapid depletion of natural forests, caused by the increased use of timber for powering the new industries, led to demands for forest conservation. The United States also saw many of its great forests razed, huge tracts of land leveled for open-pit mining and quarrying, and increased disease with the rise of air pollution from the smokestacks of factories, home chimneys, and engine exhaust. Much of the land damage occurred at the same time as a dramatic depletion of wildlife, including elk, antelope, deer, bison, and other animals of the Great Plains. Some types of bear, cougar, and wolf became extinct, as did several kinds of birds, such as the passenger pigeon. In the latter half of the nineteenth century, the U.S. government set up a commission to develop scientific management of fisheries, established the first national park (Yellowstone), and set aside the first forest reserves. The modern conservation movement grew out of these early steps.

In 1891, the area surrounding Yellowstone became a U.S. forest reserve, inaugurating the country's system of national forests. States also established parks and forests for wilderness conservation. Parks and forests became a place where people, especially urban dwellers, could acquaint themselves with the natural settings of their ancestors. Naturalists, employed by the government, institutions of higher education, and various private concerns, were involved not only in preserving and exploring the natural reserves but also in educating the public about the remaining wilderness.

Controversy over the proper role of U.S. parks and forests began soon after their creation (and continues to this day), as the value of these natural areas for logging, recreation, and other human activities conflicted with the ecological need for preservation. Among the advocates of strict preservation was John Muir, founder of the Sierra Club. President Theodore Roosevelt, also a strong supporter of the conservation movement, believed nevertheless in limited industrial projects, such as dams, within the wilderness areas. Despite the controversy, the system of national parks and forests expanded throughout the twentieth century. Today, the Agriculture and Interior Departments, and to a lesser extent the Department of Defense, have conservation responsibilities for soil, forests, grasslands, water, wildlife, and federally owned land.

In the 1960s and early 1970s, the hazards posed by pollution to both humans and the environment highlighted the importance of nature preservation and public education. Federal agencies were established, including the Environmental Protection Agency (EPA), Council on Environmental Quality, and National Oceanic and Atmospheric Administration (NOAA); and crucial legislation was passed, including the Wilderness Act (1964) and the Endangered Species Act (1969). Naturalists are closely involved with these conservation efforts and others, and it is their responsibility to communicate to the public the importance of maintaining diverse ecosystems and to help restore or balance ecosystems under threat.

Nature of the Work

Because of the impact of human populations on the environment, no area, particularly in the United States, is truly "wild." The land and the animal populations require human intervention to help battle against the human encroachment that is damaging or hindering the wildlife. Naturalists work to help the wildlife maintain or improve their hold in the world.

The work can be directly involved in maintaining individual populations of animals or plants, or overseeing whole ecosystems, or promoting the work of those who are directly involved in the maintenance of the ecosystem. Fish and wildlife officers (or fish and game wardens) work to preserve and restore the animal populations, including migratory birds that may only be part of the environment temporarily. Wildlife managers and range conservationists oversee the combination of plants and animals in their territory.

Fish and wildlife officers and wardens study, assist, and help regulate the populations of fish, hunted animals, and protected animals throughout the United States. They may work directly in the parks and reserves or they may oversee a region within a particular state, even if there are no park lands there. Fish and game wardens control the hunting and fishing of wild populations to make sure that the populations are not overharvested during a season. They monitor the populations of each species off-season as well to make sure the species is thriving but is not overpopulating and running the risk of starvation or territory damage.   Most people hear about the fish and game wardens when a population of animals has overgrown its territory and needs either to be culled (selectively hunted) or moved.   Usually this is the deer population, but it can also be for predator animals such as the coyote or fox, or scavenger animals such as the raccoon.   Because of the controversial practice of culling animal populations, the local press usually covers these stories when they occur.

The other common time to hear about wildlife wardens is when poaching is uncovered locally.   Poaching can be hunting or fishing an animal out of season, or hunting or fishing a protected animal.   Although we think of poachers in the African plains hunting lions and elephants, poaching is common in the United States for animals such as mountain lions, brown bears, eagles, and wolves.   Game wardens target and arrest poachers; besides possible prison sentences, punishment can include steep fines.

Fish and wildlife officers work to maintain refuges, but they are also responsible for educating the public, particularly about the controversial practices involved in maintaining a population; they may have outreach and demonstration programs that help inform the public about what the U.S. Fish and Wildlife Service does and what the public can do to help.   Programs may include public days for helping to clean up, restore, or repair wild areas.

Wildlife managers and range managers and conservationists work to maintain the plant and animal life in a given area.   Wildlife managers can work in small local parks or enormous national parks.   Range managers work on ranges that have a combination of domestic livestock and wild population.   The United States federal government has leased and permitted farmers to graze and raise livestock on federally held ranges, although this program is under increasing attack by outside conservationists.   Range managers must ensure that both the domestic and wild populations are living side-by-side successfully.   They make sure that the population of predatory wild animals does not increase enough to deplete the livestock, and that the livestock does not overgraze the land, and eliminate essential food for the wild animals.   Range managers and conservationists must test soil and water for nutrients and pollution, count plant and animal populations in every season, and keep in contact with farmers using the land for reports of attack on livestock or presence of disease in either the livestock or the wildlife.

Wildlife managers also balance the needs of the humans using or traveling through the land they supervise and the animals that live in or travel through that same land.   They keep track of the populations of animals and plants and provide food and water when it is lacking naturally.   This may involve air-drops of hay and grain during winter months to deer, moose, or elk populations in remote reaches of a national forest, or digging and filling a water reservoir for animals during a drought.

Naturalists in all these positions often have administrative duties such as supervising staff members and volunteers, raising funds (particularly for independent nonprofit organizations), writing grant applications, taking and keeping records and statistics, and public relations. They may write articles for local or national publications to inform and educate the public about their location or a specific project. They may be interviewed by journalists for reports concerning their site or their work.

Nature walks are often given to groups as a way of educating people about the land and the work that goes into restoring and maintaining it. Tourists, school children, amateur conservationists and naturalists, social clubs, and retirees commonly attend these walks. On a nature walk, the naturalist may point out specific plants and animals, identify rocks, and discuss soil composition or the natural history of the area (including special environmental strengths and problems). The naturalist may even discuss the indigenous people of the area, especially in terms of how they adapted to the unique aspects of their particular environment. Because such a variety of topics may be brought up, the naturalist must be an environmental generalist, familiar with such subjects as biology, botany, geology, geography, meteorology, anthropology, and history.

Demonstrations, exhibits, and classes are ways that the naturalist can educate the public about the environment. For example, to help children understand oil spills, the naturalist may set up a simple demonstration showing that oil and water do not mix. Sometimes the natural setting already provides an exhibit for the naturalist. Dead fish, birds, and other animals found in a park may help demonstrate the natural life cycle and the process of decomposition. Instruction may also be given on outdoor activities, such as hiking and camping. "Low-impact camping" involves leaving as few traces of human presence in nature as possible. For example, the naturalist instructs people on how to pack out their trash, bury the coals of their fires, and return the campsite to its most natural state by redistributing twigs, sticks, and grasses across bare dirt and replacing any stones or logs they may have moved to create a fire circle. In some parks, low-impact camping is required, so every group must be educated about how to leave the land as they found it.

For some naturalists, preparing educational materials is a large part of their job. Brochures, fact-sheets, pamphlets, and newsletters may be written for people visiting the park or nature center. Materials might also be sent to area residents in an effort to gain public support.

One aspect of protecting any natural area involves communicating facts and debunking myths about how to respect the area and the flora and fauna that inhabit it. Another aspect involves tending managed areas to promote a diversity of plants and animals. This may mean introducing trails and footpaths that provide easy, yet noninvasive, access for the public; it may mean cordoning off an area to prevent foot traffic from ruining a patch of rare moss; or it may mean instigating a letter-writing campaign to drum up support for legislation that would protect a specific area, plant, or animal. It may be easy to get support for protecting the snowshoe rabbit; it is harder to make the public understand the need to preserve and maintain a batcave.

Some naturalists, such as directors of nature centers or conservation organizations, have massive administrative responsibilities. They might recruit volunteers and supervise staff, organize long- and short-term program goals, and handle record keeping and the budget. To raise money, naturalists may need to speak publicly on a regular basis, write grant proposals, and organize and attend scheduled fundraising activities and community meetings. Naturalists also try to increase public awareness and support by writing press releases and organizing public workshops, conferences, seminars, meetings, and hearings. In general, naturalists must be available as a resource or advisor to the community.

Requirements

High school students interested in the field should consider taking a number of basic science courses, including biology and chemistry. Botany courses and clubs are helpful, since they give you direct experience with monitoring plant growth and health. Animal care experience, usually obtained through volunteer work, also is helpful.

An undergraduate degree in environmental, physical, or natural sciences is generally the minimum educational requirement for becoming a naturalist. Common college majors are biology, forestry, wildlife management, natural resource and park management, natural resources, botany, zoology, chemistry, natural history, and environmental science. Course work in economics, history, anthropology, English, international studies, and communications is also helpful.

Graduate education is increasingly required for employment as a naturalist, particularly for upper level positions. A master's in natural science or natural resources is the minimum for supervisory or administrative roles in many of the nonprofit agencies, and several positions require either a doctorate or several years of experience in the field. For positions in agencies with international sites, work abroad is also required, and can be obtained through volunteer positions such as those with the Peace Corps, or in paid positions assisting in site administration and management.

In the late 1990s, there were 85 colleges and universities in the United States offering undergraduate degrees in wildlife management. There were 79 bachelor degree programs in parks management and 113 in environmental biology. However, there were only 41 graduate programs in fish, game, and wildlife management, and 15 programs covering range sciences.

Those considering the field should like working outdoors, as most naturalists spend the majority of their time outside, in all kinds of weather. But along with the desire to work in and with the natural world, the naturalist needs to be capable of communicating with the human world as well. Excellent writing skills are necessary for preparing educational materials and grant proposals. It is especially important that naturalists enjoy working with people.

For people working in the field, seemingly unrelated skills such as engine repair and basic carpentry can be essential to managing a post. Because of the remote locations of many of the work sites, self-sufficiency in operating and maintaining the equipment allows the staff to lose fewer days to equipment breakdown.

Opportunities for Experience and Exploration

One of the best ways to learn about the job of a naturalist is to volunteer at one of the many national and state parks or nature centers. These institutions often recruit volunteers for outdoor work. College students, for example, are sometimes hired to work as summer or part-time nature guides. Outdoor recreation and training organizations, such as Outward Bound and the National Outdoor Leadership School (NOLS), are especially good resources. Most volunteer positions, though, require a high-school diploma and some college credit.

Students should also consider college internship programs. In addition, conservation programs and organizations throughout the country and the world can offer further opportunities for volunteer work in a wide variety of areas, including working with the public, giving lectures and guided tours, and working with others to build or maintain an ecosystem. For more continuous, up-to-date information, you can subscribe to one of several newsletters that post internship and job positions. Environmental Careers World and Environmental Career Opportunities are two newsletters to look for. Many of the organizations hiring naturalists also post their openings on their Web sites. The federal government maintains a job board at http://www.usajobs.opm.gov, so the diligent applicant can keep up on new listings without a subscription.

Methods of Entering

For park employees, the usual method of entry is through part-time or seasonal employment for the first several jobs, and then moving into a full-time position. Because it is difficult to get experience before completing a college degree, and because seasonal employment is common, students interested in this career path should prepare to seek supplemental income for their first few years in the field.

International experience is helpful with agencies that work beyond the U.S. borders. This can be through Peace Corps or other volunteer organizations that work with local populations on land and habitat management or restoration. Other volunteer experience is available through local restoration programs on sites in your area. Organizations such as the Nature Conservancy, Open Lands, and many others buy land to restore, and these organizations rely extensively on volunteer labor for stewarding and working the land. Rescue and release centers work with injured and abandoned wildlife to rerelease them. Opportunities at these centers can include banding wild animals for tracking, working with injured or adolescent animals for release training, and adapting unreleasable animals to educational programs and presentations.

Advancement

Although some naturalists find entry-level, year-round positions, many begin by working in seasonal jobs. To work as a naturalist throughout the year, some may need to move from one seasonal job to the next. Naturalists often receive on-the-job training.

In some settings, such as small nature centers, there may be little room for advancement. In larger organizations experience and additional education can lead to increased responsibility and pay. Among the higher-level positions is that of director, who handles supervisory, administrative, and public relations tasks.

Advancement into upper level management and supervisory positions usually requires a graduate degree, although people with a graduate degree and no work experience will still have to start in nearly entry-level positions. So you can either work a few years and then return to school to get an advanced degree, or complete your education and start in the same position as you would have without the degree. The advanced degree will allow you eventually to move further up in the organizational structure.

Employment Outlook

The outlook for naturalists is expected to be fair into the twenty-first century. While a growing public concern about environmental issues may cause an increased demand for naturalists, this trend could be offset by government cutbacks in nature programs. Reduced government spending on education may indirectly affect the demand for naturalists, as school districts would have less money to spend on outdoor education and recreation. Despite the limited number of available positions, the number of well-qualified applicants is expected to remain high.

Many who enter the field are so interested in a particular area or field that they return to graduate school for further study in programs such as environmental law, environmental studies, and wildlife management. Libraries and college and university placement centers are the best places to search out information on graduate programs in these and other related fields.

Earnings

Starting salaries for full-time naturalists range from about $15,000 to $22,000 per year. Some part-time workers, however, make as little as minimum wage. For some positions, housing and vehicles may be provided. Earnings vary for those with added responsibilities or advanced degrees. Field officers and supervisors will make between $25,000 and $45,000 a year, and upper management can make between $30,000 and $70,000, depending on the organization.

Conditions of Work

Field naturalists spend a majority of their working hours outdoors. Depending on the location, the naturalist must work in a wide variety of weather conditions, from frigid cold to sweltering heat to torrential rain. Remote sites are common, and long periods of working either in isolation or in small teams is not uncommon for field research and management. Heavy lifting, hauling, working with machinery and hand tools, digging, planting, harvesting, tracking, marking—these duties may fall to the naturalist working in the field. One wildlife manager in Montana spent every daylight hour for several days in a row literally running up and down snow covered mountains trying to tranquilize and collar a mountain lion. This can be a physically demanding job.

Indoor work includes scheduling, planning, and classroom teaching. Data-gathering and maintaining logs and records is a part of many jobs. Naturalists may be required to attend and speak at local community meetings. They may have to read detailed legislative bills to analyze the impact of legislation before it becomes law.

Those in supervisory positions, such as directors, are often busy with administrative and organizational tasks, so they may spend little of their work day outdoors. Work that includes guided tours and walks through nature areas is frequently seasonal and usually dependent on daily visitors.

Full-time naturalists usually work about thirty-five to forty hours per week. Overtime is usually required, and for those naturalists working in areas visited by campers, camping season is extremely busy and can require much overtime. Wildlife and range managers may be on call during storms and severe weather. Seasonal work such as burn season for land managers and stewards may require overtime and frequent weekend work.

Naturalists have special occupational hazards, such as working with helicopters, small airplanes, all-terrain vehicles, and other modes of transport through rugged landscapes, into remote regions. Adverse weather conditions and working in rough terrain make illness and injury more likely. Naturalists must be able to get along with the variety of people using the area, and may encounter armed individuals who are poaching or otherwise violating the law.

Naturalists also have a number of unique benefits. Most prominent is the chance to live and work in some of the most beautiful places in the world. For many individuals, the lower salaries are offset by the recreational and life-style opportunities afforded by living and working in such scenic areas. In general, occupational stress is low, and most naturalists appreciate the opportunity to continually learn about and work to improve the environment.

Sources of Additional Information

This organization offers environmental expeditions:

Earthwatch Expeditions, Inc.
319 Arlington Street
Watertown, MA 02272
Tel: 617-926-8200

This organization offers internship opportunities for current college students and recent graduates. It also sponsors an annual career conference and fair and produces The New Complete Guide to Environmental Careers. Contact:

Environmental Careers Organization
286 Congress Street, Third Floor
Boston, MA 02210-1038
Tel: 617-426-4375

This group offers internships and fellowships for college and graduate students with an interest in environmental issues such as environmental justice, indigenous peoples' rights, jobs and the environment, and trade. Contact:

Friends of the Earth
218 D Street, SE
Washington, DC 20003
Tel: 202-544-2600

This group has an international computer network called EcoNet that features electronic bulletin boards on environmental issues, services, events, news, and job listings. Contact them directly at:

Institute for Global Communication
18 DeBoom Street
San Francisco, CA 94107
Tel: 415-442-0220
Email: econet@igc.org
WWW: http://www.econet.org

National Wildlife Federation
8925 Leesburg Pike
Vienna, VA 22184
Tel: 718-790-4000
WWW: http://www.igc.apc.org/nwf

Park Rangers

	School Subjects
Earth science	
Geography/Social studies	
Geology	
History	
Speech	

	Personal Interests
Camping/Hiking	
The Environment	
Helping people: personal service	
Reading/Books	
Teaching	

	Work Environment
Primarily outdoors	
Primarily multiple locations	

	Minimum Education Level
Bachelor's degree	

	Salary Range
$20,000 to $30,000+	

	Certification or Licensing
None	

	Outlook
Little change or more slowly than average	

	DOT
169	

	GOE
04.02.03	

	NOC
2224	

Definition

Park rangers enforce laws and regulations in national, state, and county parks. They help care for and maintain parks as well as inform, guide, and ensure the safety of park visitors.

History

The National Park System in the United States was created by Congress in 1872 when Yellowstone National Park was created. The National Park Service (NPS) is a bureau of the U.S. Department of the Interior. It was created in 1916 to preserve, protect, and manage the national, cultural, historical, and recreational areas of the National Park System. At that time, the park system contained less than one million acres. Today the country's national parks cover more than eighty million acres of mountains, plains, deserts, swamps, historic sites, lakeshores, forests, rivers, battlefields, memorials, archeological properties, and recreation areas.

All NPS areas are given one of the following designations: National Park, National Historical Park, National Battlefield, National Battlefield Park, National Battlefield Site, National Military Site, National Memorial, National Historic Site, National Monument, National Preserve, National Seashore, National Parkway, National Lakeshore, National Reserve, National River, National Wild and Scenic River, National Recreation Area, or just Park. (The White House in Washington, DC, for example, which is administered by the NPS, is officially a Park.)

To protect the fragile, irreplaceable resources located in these areas, and to protect the millions of visitors who climb, ski, hike, boat, fish, and otherwise explore them, the National Park Service employs park rangers. State and county parks employ rangers to perform similar tasks.

Nature of the Work

Park rangers have a wide variety of duties that range from conservation efforts to bookkeeping. Their first responsibility is, however, safety. Rangers who work in parks with treacherous terrain, dangerous wildlife, or severe weather must make sure hikers, campers, and backpackers follow outdoor safety codes. They often require visitors to register at park offices so that rangers will know when someone does not return from a hike or climb and may be hurt. Rangers often participate in search-and-rescue missions for visitors who are lost or injured in parks. In mountainous or forested regions they may use helicopters or horses for searches.

Many rangers patrol park areas to monitor the use of park land by visitors. In mountainous, snowy areas, snow rangers patrol on skis or snowmobiles. Rangers patrolling in air boats skim the waters of the Everglades. Rangers are trained in first aid and rescue procedures and have saved the lives of many visitors who were careless in the outdoors or who were injured or lost due to bad weather or darkness.

Rangers also are concerned with protecting parks from inappropriate use and other threats from humans. They register vehicles and collect parking and registration fees, which are used to help maintain roads and facilities. They enforce the laws, regulations, and policies of the parks, patrolling to prevent vandalism, theft, and harm to wildlife. Rangers may arrest and evict people who violate these laws. Some of their efforts to conserve and protect park resources include keeping jeeps and other motorized vehicles off sand dunes and other fragile lands. They make sure visitors do not litter, pollute water, chop down trees for firewood, or start unsafe campfires that could lead to catastrophic forest fires. When forest fires do start, rangers often help with the dangerous, arduous task of putting them out.

Park rangers carry out various tasks associated with the management of the natural resources encompassed within our National Park System. An important aspect of this responsibility is the care and management of both native and exotic animal species found within the boundaries of the parks. Duties may include conducting basic research, as well as disseminating information about the reintroduction of native animal populations, and the protection of the natural habitat that supports the animals.

Rangers also help with conservation, research, and ecology efforts that are not connected to visitors' use of the park. They may study wildlife behavior patterns, for example, by tagging and following certain animals. In this way they can chart the animals' migration patterns, assess the animals' impact on the park's ecosystem, and determine whether the park should take measures to control or encourage certain wildlife populations.

The extent and type of animal care, of course, varies greatly among the different park sites. At the George Washington Birthplace National Monument in Virginia, for example, farm animals are raised. "We have some unique breeds that cannot be found elsewhere, but that were here when George Washington was born," Chief Ranger Larry Trombello noted. The most notable of these nearly extinct breeds are the Hog Island sheep; the red milking devon, a cow which settlers brought here from England in the 1700s; and the Ossabaw Island hog. Rangers care for these and other more ordinary farm animals in several pastures.

At Guadalupe Mountains National Park in western Texas, horses and mules are kept to help the rangers do their work and to get into areas of the park where an automobile cannot go. They are also used for search-and-rescue missions, when visitors are lost or injured in an inaccessible part of the park. Rangers feed and take care of the horses and mules; but as far as wild animals are concerned, at this and all NPS sites, the rule is to let nature take its course. No care is given and no hunting is allowed. Richard McCamant, chief of interpreters and visitor service at Guadalupe, said that if an animal is injured, it is either sent to a facility where it can get the proper care, or is put out of its misery if it is too late for care.

Some rangers study plant life and may work with conservationists to reintroduce native or endangered species. They measure the quality of water and air in the park to monitor and mitigate the effects of pollution and other threats emanating from sources outside park boundaries.

In addition, park rangers help visitors enjoy and experience parks. In historical and other cultural parks, such as the Alamo in San Antonio, Independence Hall in Philadelphia, or the Lincoln Home in Springfield, Illinois, rangers give lectures and provide guided tours explaining the history and significance of the site. In natural parks, they may lecture on conservation topics, provide information about plants and animals in the park, and take visitors on interpretive walks, pointing out the area's flora, fauna, and geological characteristics. At a Civil War battlefield park such as Gettysburg National Military Park in Pennsylvania or Vicksburg National Military Park in Mississippi, they explain to visitors what happened at that site during the Civil War and its implications for our country.

Park rangers are also indispensable to the management and administration of parks. They issue permits to visitors and vehicles and help plan the recreational activities in parks. They are involved with planning and managing park budgets. They keep records and compile statistics concerning weather conditions, resource conservation activities, and the number of park visitors.

Many rangers supervise other workers in the parks—those who build and maintain park facilities, work part time or seasonally, or operate concession facilities. Rangers often have their own park-maintenance responsibilities, such as trail building, landscaping, and caring for visitor centers.

In some parks, rangers are specialists in certain areas of park protection, safety, or management. For example, in areas with heavy snowfalls and a high incidence of avalanches, experts in avalanche control and snow safety are designated as *snow rangers*. They monitor snow conditions and patrol park areas to make sure visitors are not lost in snow slides.

Requirements

High school students who wish to prepare for the necessary college course-load should take courses in earth science, mathematics, English, and speech. Any classes or activities that deal with plant and animal life, the weather, geography, and interacting with others will be helpful.

Employment as a federal or state park ranger requires either a college degree or a specific amount of education and experience. Approximately two hundred colleges and universities offer bachelor's degree programs in park management and park recreation. To meet employment requirements, students in other relevant college programs must accumulate at least twenty-four semester hours of academic credit in park recreation and management, history, behavioral sciences, forestry, botany, geology, or other applicable subject areas.

Without a degree, applicants need three years of experience in parks or conservation and must show they understand what is required in park work. In addition, they must demonstrate good communications skills. A combination of education and experience can also fulfill job requirements, with one academic year of study equalling nine months of experience. Also, the orientation and training a ranger receives on the job may be supplemented with formal training courses.

Rangers need skills in protecting forests, parks, and wildlife or in interpreting natural or historical resources. Law enforcement and management skills are also important. Rangers who wish to move into management positions may need graduate degrees. Approximately fifty universities offer master's degrees in park recreation and management, and sixteen have doctoral programs.

The right kind of person to fill a park ranger position believes in the importance of the country's park resources and the mission of the park system. People who enjoy working outdoors—independently and with others—may enjoy park ranger work. Rangers need self-confidence, patience, and the ability to stay level-headed during emergencies. Those who participate in rescues need courage, physical stamina, and endurance, while those who deal with visitors need tact, sincerity, personable natures, and a sense of humor. A sense of camaraderie among fellow rangers also can add to the enjoyment of being a park ranger.

Opportunities for Experience and Exploration

Persons interested in exploring park ranger work may wish to apply for part-time or seasonal work in national, state, or county parks. Such workers usually perform maintenance and other unskilled tasks, but they have opportunities to observe park rangers and talk with them about their work. Interested persons also may wish to work as volunteers. Many park research activities, study projects, and rehabilitation efforts are conducted by volunteer groups affiliated with universities or conservation organizations, and these activities can provide insight into the work done by park rangers.

Methods of Entering

Many workers enter national park ranger jobs after working part time or seasonally at different parks. These workers often work at information desks or in fire control or law enforcement positions. Some help maintain trails, collect trash, or perform forestry activities. Persons interested in applying for park ranger jobs with the federal government should write to their local Federal Job Information Center or the Federal Office of Personnel Management in Washington, DC, for application information. Those people seeking jobs in state parks should write to state parks departments for information.

Advancement

Nearly all rangers start in entry-level positions, which means that nearly all higher-level openings are filled by the promotion of current workers. Entry-level rangers may move into positions as district ranger or park manager, or they may become specialists in resource management or park planning.

Cheryl Matthews began her career at Yellowstone National Park as a dispatcher in the communications center before moving up to a clerk-typist position in public affairs. She is now a ranger with the title of Assistant Chief of Public Affairs, and credits the Yellowstone staff for making that possible. "I had wonderful supervisors," she said, "who always encouraged me and gave me the opportunity to learn and grow."

Rangers who show management skills and become park managers may move into administrative positions in the district, regional, or national headquarters. With more responsibility comes higher pay.

Employment Outlook

Park ranger jobs are scarce, and competition for them is fierce. The U.S. Park Service has reported that the ratio of applicants to available positions is sometimes as high as one hundred to one. As a result, applicants should attain the greatest number and widest variety of applicable skills possible. They may wish to study subjects they can use in other fields: forestry, conservation, wildlife management, history, and natural sciences, for example.

The scarcity of openings is expected to continue indefinitely. Job seekers, therefore, may wish to apply for outdoor work with agencies other than the National Park Service, including other federal land and resource management agencies and similar state and local agencies. These agencies usually have more openings.

Earnings

Rangers in the National Park Service are employed by the U.S. Department of the Interior. Beginning rangers are usually hired at the GS-5 grade level, with a salary of around $20,000. More experienced or educated rangers may enter the Park Service at the GS-9 level, which pays approximately $30,000 to start. The government may provide housing to rangers who work in remote areas.

Rangers in state parks work for the state government. They receive comparable salaries and benefits, including paid vacations, sick leave, paid holidays, health and life insurance, and pension plans.

Conditions of Work

Rangers work in parks all over the country, from the Okefenokee Swamp in Florida to the Rocky Mountains of Colorado. They work in the mountains and forests of Hawaii, Alaska, and California, and in urban and suburban parks throughout the United States.

National park rangers are hired to work forty-hour weeks, but their hours can be long and irregular, with a great deal of overtime. They may receive extra pay or time off for working overtime. Some rangers are on call twenty-four hours a day for emergencies. During the peak tourist seasons, rangers work longer hours. Although many rangers work in offices, many also work outside in all kinds of climates and weather, and most work in a combination of the two settings. Workers may be called upon to risk their own health to rescue injured visitors in cold, snow, rain, and darkness. Rangers in Alaska must adapt to long daylight hours in the summer and short daylight hours in the winter. Working outdoors in beautiful surroundings, however, can be wonderfully stimulating and rewarding for the right kind of worker.

Terry Winschel, who is now a historian at Vicksburg National Military Park, but began his career as a ranger, says that "stewardship of our national treasures is a rich and rewarding career—to me, it is a career of which dreams are made." Larry Blake, at the Lincoln Home National Historic Site, says that he was particularly drawn to the opportunity "to teach our history to young people." He cares about what the Park Service stands for—working to preserve valuable natural and historical resources and doing something for the future.

Sources of Additional Information

National Association of State Park Directors
9894 East Holden Place
Tucson, AZ 85748
Tel: 520-298-4924

National Recreation and Park Association
22377 Belmont Ridge Road
Ashburn, VA 20148-4510
Tel: 703-858-0784
WWW: http://www.nrpa.org

National Parks and Conservation Association
1776 Massachusetts Avenue, NW
Washington, DC 20036
Tel: 202-223-6722
WWW: http://www.npca.org/npca

Student Conservation Association
PO Box 550
Charlestown, NC 03603-0550
Tel: 603-543-1700
WWW: http://www.sca-inc.org

U.S. Department of the Interior

National Park Service
1849 C Street, NW
Washington, DC 20240
Tel: 202-208-4648
WWW: http://www.nps.gov/nps

Pet Groomers

Definition

Pet groomers comb, cut, trim, and shape the fur of all types of dogs and cats. They comb out the animal's fur and trim the hair to the proper style for the size and breed. They also trim the animal's nails, bathe it, and dry its hair. In the process, they check for flea or tick infestation and any visible health problems. In order to perform these grooming tasks, the pet groomer must be able to calm the animal down and gain its confidence.

History

As long as dog has been man's best friend, humans have been striving to keep their animal companions healthy and happy. Pets are often considered members of the family and are treated as such. Just as parents take their children to the doctor for vaccinations and to the barber for haircuts, pets are often treated to regular veterinarian visits and grooming services.

An increasingly urban society and higher standards of living can both be considered significant factors in the growing number of professional grooming establishments in this country. City-dwellers who live in small apartments have less space to groom their pets than their farm-dwelling forefathers had. Many busy professionals have neither the time nor the inclination to learn the proper techniques and purchase the tools needed for grooming. Additionally, many apartment and condominium buildings have regulations to which pet owners must adhere in order to ensure the safety and comfort of tenants. In compact living quarters, people don't want to encounter smelly pups in the hallway. Also, the rise of multiple-income families and an increased standard of living gives animal aficionados the disposable income to pamper their pets with professional grooming services.

Groomers are also called upon to tend to more exotic pets these days, such as ferrets, birds, and reptiles. New developments in animal grooming include high performance clippers and cutting tools and more humane restraining devices. Current trends toward specialized services include perfuming, powdering, styling, and even massage, aromatherapy and tattooing for pets!

Nature of the Work

Although all dogs and cats benefit from regular grooming, shaggy, longhaired dogs give pet groomers the bulk of their business. Some types of dogs need regular grooming for their standard appearance; among this group are poodles, schnauzers, cocker spaniels, and many types of terriers. Show dogs, or dogs that are shown in competition, are groomed frequently. Before beginning grooming, the dog groomer talks with the owner to find out the style of cut that the dog is to have. The dog groomer also relies on experience to determine how a particular breed of dog is supposed to look.

The dog groomer places the animal on a grooming table. To keep the dog steady during the clipping, a nylon collar or noose, which hangs from an adjustable pole attached to the grooming table, is slipped around its neck. The dog groomer talks to the dog or uses other techniques to keep the animal calm and gain its trust. If the dog doesn't calm down but snaps and bites instead, the groomer may have to muzzle it. If a dog is completely unmanageable, the dog groomer may ask the owner to have the dog tranquilized by a veterinarian before grooming.

After calming the dog down, the groomer brushes it and tries to untangle its hair. If the dog's hair is very overgrown or is very shaggy such as an English sheepdog's, the groomer may have to cut away part of its coat with scissors before beginning any real grooming. Brushing the coat is good for both longhaired and shorthaired dogs as brushing removes shedding hair and dead skin. It also neatens the coat so the groomer can tell from the shape and proportions of the dog how to cut its hair in the most attractive way. Hair that is severely matted is actually painful to the animal because the mats pull at the animal's skin. Having these mats removed is necessary to the animal's health and comfort.

Once the dog is brushed, the groomer cuts and shapes the dog's coat with electric clippers. Next, the dog's ears are cleaned and its nails are trimmed. The groomer must take care not to cut the nails too short because they may bleed and cause the dog pain. If the nails do bleed, a special powder is applied to stop the bleeding. The comfort of the animal is an important concern for the groomer.

The dog is then given a bath, sometimes by a worker known as a dog bather. The dog is lowered into a stainless steel tub, sprayed with warm water, scrubbed with a special shampoo, and rinsed. This may be repeated several times if the dog is very dirty. The dog groomer has special chemicals that can be used to deodorize a dog that has encountered a skunk or has gone for a swim in foul water. If a dog has fleas or ticks, the dog groomer treats them at this stage by soaking the wet coat with a solution to kill the insects. This toxic solution must be kept out of the dog's eyes, ears, and nose, which may be cleaned more carefully with a sponge or washcloth. A hot oil treatment may also be applied to condition the dog's coat.

The groomer dries the dog after bathing, either with a towel, hand-held electric blower, or in a drier cage with electric blow driers. Poodles and some other types of dogs have their coats fluff-dried, then scissored for the final pattern or style. Poodles, which at one time were the mainstay of the dog grooming business, generally take the longest to groom because of their intricate clipping pattern. Most dogs can be groomed in about ninety minutes, although grooming may take several hours for shaggier breeds whose coats are badly matted and overgrown.

More and more cats, especially longhaired breeds, are now being taken to pet groomers. The procedure for cats is the same as for dogs, although cats are not dipped when bathed. As the dog or cat is groomed, the groomer checks to be sure there are no signs of disease in the animal's eyes, ears, skin, or coat. If there are any abnormalities, such as bald patches or skin lesions, the groomer tells the owner and may recommend that a veterinarian check the animal. The groomer may also give the owner tips on animal hygiene.

Pet owners and those in pet care generally have respect for pet groomers who do a good job and treat animals well. Many people, especially those who raise show dogs, grow to rely on particular pet groomers to do a perfect job each time. Pet groomers can earn satisfaction from taking a shaggy, unkempt animal and transforming it into a beautiful creature. On the other hand, some owners may unfairly blame the groomer if the animal becomes ill while in the groomer's care or for some malady or condition that is not the groomer's fault.

Because they deal with both the pets and their owners, pet groomers can find their work both challenging and rewarding. One owner of a grooming business asserts, "Nothing feels better than developing a relationship with pets and their owners. It's almost like they become an extended part of the family. When working with living animals you accept the responsibility of caring for them to the best of your ability, and the rewards are great. I don't think that can be said of a mechanic or furnace repairman."

Requirements

A high school diploma generally is not required for people working as pet groomers. A diploma or GED certificate, however, can be a great asset to people who would like to advance within their present company or move to other careers in animal care that require more training, such as *veterinary technicians*. Useful courses include English, business math, general science, anatomy and physiology, health, zoology, psychology, bookkeeping, office management, typing, art, and first aid.

Presently, state licensing or certification is not required, and there are no established labor unions for pet groomers. To start a grooming salon or other business, a license is needed from the city or town in which a person plans to practice.

The primary qualification for a person who wants to work with pets is a love of animals. Animals can sense when someone does not like them or is afraid of them. A person needs certain skills in order to work with nervous, aggressive, or fidgety animals. They must be patient with the animals, able to gain their respect, and enjoy giving the animals a lot of love and attention. Persistence and endurance are also helpful as grooming one animal can take several hours of strenuous work. Groomers should enjoy working with their hands and have good eyesight and manual dexterity to accurately cut a clipping pattern.

A person interested in pet grooming can be trained for the field in one of three ways: enrolling in a pet grooming school; working in a pet shop or kennel and learning on the job; or reading one of the many books on pet grooming and practicing on his or her own pet.

To enroll in most pet grooming schools, a person must be at least seventeen years old and fond of animals. Previous experience in pet grooming can sometimes be applied for course credits. Students study a wide range of topics including the basics of bathing, brushing, and clipping, the care of ears and nails, coat and skin conditions, animal anatomy terminology and sanitation. They also study customer relations, which is very important for those who plan to operate their own shops. During training, students practice their techniques on actual animals, which people bring in for grooming at a discount rate.

Students can also learn pet grooming while working for a grooming shop, kennel, animal hospital, or veterinarian's office. They usually begin with tasks such as shampooing dogs and cats, and trimming their nails, then gradually work their way up to brushing and basic hair cuts. With experience, they may learn more difficult cuts and use these skills to earn more pay or start their own business.

The essentials of pet grooming can also be learned from any of several good books available on grooming. These books contain all the information a person needs to know to start his or her own pet grooming business, including the basic cuts, bathing and handling techniques, and type of equipment needed. Still, many of the finer points of grooming, such as the more complicated cuts and various safety precautions, are best learned while working under an experienced groomer. There still is no substitute for on-the-job training and experience.

Opportunities for Experience and Exploration

To find out if they are suited for a job in pet grooming, students should familiarize themselves with animals as much as possible. This can be done in many ways, starting with the proper care of the family pet. Students can also offer to tend to the pets of friends and neighbors to see how well they handle unfamiliar animals. Youth organizations such as the Boy Scouts, Girl Scouts, and 4-H Clubs sponsor projects that give members the chance to raise and care for animals. Students also may do part-time or volunteer work caring for animals at an animal hospital, kennel, pet shop, animal shelter, nature center, or zoo.

Methods of Entering

The best ways for most people to gain a thorough knowledge of dog grooming is through hands-on experience and enrollment in an accredited pet grooming course or a pet grooming school. The National Dog Groomers Association of America (NDGAA) provides a referral listing of approximately forty dog grooming schools throughout the United States to persons who send a stamped, self-addressed envelope. Three schools of dog grooming are recognized by the National Association of Trade and Technical Schools (NATTS): the Pedigree Professional School of Dog Grooming, the New York School of Dog Grooming (three branches), and the Nash Academy of Animal Arts. Many other dog grooming schools advertise in dog and pet magazines. It is important for students to choose an accredited, licensed school in order to increase both their employment opportunities and professional knowledge.

Graduates from dog grooming schools can take advantage of the school's job placement services. Generally, there are more job openings than qualified groomers to fill them, so new graduates may have several job offers to consider. These schools learn of job openings in all parts of the United States and are usually happy to contact prospective employers and write letters of introduction for graduates.

The NDGAA also promotes professional identification through membership and certification testing throughout the United States and Canada. The NDGAA offers continuing education, accredited workshops, certification testing, seminars, insurance programs, a job placement program, membership directory, and other services and products. Other associations of interest to dog groomers are the Humane Society of the United States and the United Kennel Club. Because dog groomers are concerned with the health and safety of the animals they service, membership in groups that promote and protect animal welfare is very common.

Other sources of job information include the classified ads of daily newspapers and listings in dog and pet magazines. Job leads may be available from private or state employment agencies or from referrals of salon or kennel owners. People looking for work should phone or send letters to prospective employers, inform them of their qualifications, and, if invited, visit their establishments.

Advancement

Pet groomers who work for other people may advance to a more responsible position such as office manager or dog trainer. If a dog groomer starts his or her own shop, it may become successful enough to expand or to open branch offices or area franchises. Skilled groomers may want to work for a dog grooming school as an instructor, possibly advancing to a job as a school director, placement officer, or other type of administrator.

The pet industry is booming, so there are many avenues of advancement for groomers who like to work with pets. With more education, a groomer may get a job as a veterinary technician or assistant at a shelter or animal hospital. Those who like to train dogs may open obedience schools, train guide dogs, work with field and hunting dogs, or even train stunt and movie dogs. People can also open their own kennels, breeding and pedigree services, gaming dog businesses, or pet supply distribution firms. Each of these requires specialized knowledge and experience, so additional study, education, and work is often needed.

Employment Outlook

The demand for skilled dog groomers has grown faster than average, and is expected to continue through the year 2006. The NDGAA estimates that more than 30,000 dog groomers are currently employed, and expects that more than 3,000 new groomers will be needed every year during the next decade.

Every year more people are keeping dogs and cats as pets. They are spending more money to pamper their animals, but often don't have enough free time or the inclination to groom their pets themselves. Grooming is not just a luxury for pets, however, because regular attention makes it more likely that any injury or illness will be noticed and treated.

Also, as nontraditional pets become more mainstream, innovative groomers will need to take advantage of new techniques and facilities for bringing animals other than dogs and cats into the pet salon.

Earnings

Groomers charge either by the job or the hour. If they are on the staff of a salon or work for another groomer, they get to keep 50 to 60 percent of the fees they charge. For this reason, many groomers branch off to start their own businesses. "I would never want to go back to working for someone else or giving up a commission on my groomings," says one owner-operator of a grooming business.

According to 1998 edition of *The O*Net Dictionary of Occupational Titles*, animal groomers can expect to earn $14,300 per year, while the Bureau of Labor Statistics suggests that the top ten percent of workers in the field earned more than $500 per week ($26,000 per year) in 1996. Those who own and operate their own grooming services can earn significantly more, depending on how hard they work, the clientele they service, and the economy of the area in which they work.

Groomers generally buy their own clipping equipment, including barber's shears, brushes, and clippers. A new set of equipment costs around $325; used sets cost less. Groomers employed full time at salons, grooming schools, pet shops, animal hospitals, and kennels often get a full range of benefits, including paid vacations and holidays, medical and dental insurance, and retirement pensions.

Conditions of Work

Salons, kennels, and pet shops, as well as gaming and breeding services, should be clean and well lighted, with modern equipment and clean surroundings. Establishments that do not meet these standards endanger the health of the animals that are taken there and the owners of these establishments should be reported. Groomers who are self-employed may work out of their homes. Some groomers buy vans and convert them into grooming shops. They drive them to the homes of the pets they work on, which many owners find very convenient. Those who operate these groommobiles may work on thirty or forty dogs a week, and factor their driving time and expenses into their fees.

Groomers usually work a forty-hour week and may have to work evenings or weekends. Those who own their own shops or work out of their homes, like other self-employed people, work very long hours and may have irregular schedules. One groomer points out that, "You can't just decide to call in sick when you have seven dogs scheduled to be groomed that day. We have had midnight emergency calls from clients... needing immediate help of one kind or another with their pet." Many groomers/business owners believe that the occasionally hectic schedule of the field is not always a negative aspect, since they take great pride in being able to offer personal service and care to both critters and clients.

Groomers are on their feet much of the day, and their work can get very tiring when they have to lift and restrain large animals. They must wear comfortable clothing that allows for freedom of movement, but they should also be presentable enough to deal with pet owners and other clients.

When working with any sort of animal, a person may encounter bites, scratches, strong odors, fleas, and other insects. They may have to deal with sick or bad-tempered animals. The groomer must regard every animal as a unique individual and treat it with respect. Groomers need to be careful while on the job, especially when handling flea and tick killers, which are toxic to humans (as well as the pests!).

Sources of Additional Information

The National Dog Groomers Association of America (NDGAA) publishes a newsletter for dog groomers that includes information on shows, new grooming products and techniques, and workshop and certification test sites and dates. For information and/or list of dog grooming schools across the country, send a stamped, self-addressed #10 envelope to:

National Dog Groomers Association of America, Inc.
PO Box 101
Clark, PA 16113
Tel: 724-962-2711
Email: ndga@nauticom.net
WWW: http://www.nauticom.net/www/ndga/index.html

For information on pet grooming schools and certification, contact:

New York School of Dog Grooming
248 East 34th Street
New York, NY 10016
Tel: 212-685-3776

California School of Dog Grooming
727 West San Marcos Boulevard, Suite 105A
San Marcos, CA 92069
Tel: 760-471-0787 or 800-949-3746
Email: csdg@pacbell.net
WWW: http://www.csdg.net/index1a.htm

Nash Academy of Animal Arts
857 Lane Allen Plaza
Lexington, KY 40504
Tel: 606-276-5301

For more information about grooming and related professions, contact:

Intergroom
250 East 73rd Street, Suite 4-F
New York, NY 10021-4311
Tel: 212-628-3537
Email: intergroom@aol.com
WWW: http://www.intergroom.com/

Pet Shop Workers

Business Economics	School Subjects
Helping people: personal service Selling/Making a deal	Personal Interests
Primarily indoors Primarily one location	Work Environment
High school diploma	Minimum Education Level
$12,000 to $21,000 to $30,000	Salary Range
None	Certification or Licensing
Faster than the average	Outlook

Definition

Pet shop workers, from entry-level clerks to store managers, are involved in the daily upkeep of a pet store; they sell pets and pet supplies including food, medicine, toys, carriers, and educational books and videos. They work with customers, answering questions and offering animal care advice. They keep the store, aquariums, and animal cages clean, and look after the health of the pets for sale. They also stock shelves, order products from distributors, and maintain records on the animals and products.

History

Can you imagine George Washington with a pet hamster? No? Well, there's a good reason for that—the hamster wasn't even domesticated until around 1930. But picturing George alongside his faithful steed isn't a problem at all. Just as successful horse trading was important to the development of Indian villages for thousands of years, horse trading proved a staple of American business from the first colonies to the cities of the early twentieth century.

Though the horses in the stables of the early Americans were well-loved by their owners, they weren't exactly considered "pets" or "companion animals." Horses were relied upon for transportation, industry, and farm work. But these horse traders, with their sense of business and knowledge of animal care, are early examples of the pet shop owners who found thriving business on the town squares across the developing country, alongside the apothecaries and general stores.

Though domestic cats in the United States only date from around 1750, they were first domesticated (along with lions and hyenas) around 1900 BC in Egypt. In the years before that, cats were considered sacred (perhaps explaining the royal bearing of many of today's pampered house cats!). Dogs as pets predate cats; ancient carvings and paintings depict a range of breeds, and Egyptian tomb paintings feature greyhounds and terriers.

Nature of Work

The tiny barks of the puppies being groomed in the back of the shop; the trills and whistles of the birds in their cages; the bubbling of the fish tanks-these sights and sounds combine to make a visit to the neighborhood pet store unlike any other shopping experience. But running a pet shop calls upon the same business skills required for the operation of any retail establishment. Pet shop workers are in the business to sell to customers; many pet stores employ *cashiers*, sales and marketing people, *managers*, and *bookkeepers*. *Pet shop owners* may also hire *pet groomers*, *animal caretakers*, and *animal trainers*. A pet shop must have a staff that loves animals, is knowledgeable about pets and their care, and is good with customers.

The top priorities for pet shop workers are animal care and customer care. Though the size of the pet shop will determine how many duties are assigned each worker, most pet shop workers take part in preparing the store for opening; they make sure the shop is clean, the shelves are in order, the aisles are clear, and the cash register is ready for sales. Cages and fish tanks are cleaned, and the animals are fed and watered. Though some pet shops continue to sell dogs and cats, most buyers for those kinds of animals purchase directly from breeders, or select animals from shelters and the Humane Society. Today's pet shops generally specialize in birds, fish, and small animals such as hamsters and mice. Once the animals are taken care of, the pet shop workers see to the needs of the customers. "At a small pet shop, you begin to think of your customers as your friends," says Max Paterson, a high school student who works for a pet shop in Ohio. "I once tried to count how many questions I answered in a day, and when I got past 250, I stopped."

Customers rely on pet shop workers for animal care advice, and expect them to be knowledgeable not only of the pets for sale, but of the food, medicines, and other supplies, as well. "The biggest benefits I've received from the job," Max says, "are the relationships with the customers, and the huge dictionary of tropical fish I've developed in my head."

Pet shops may offer a variety of services, including pet grooming, dog training, and animal boarding. They may also offer animal vaccinations. A store manager is often responsible for organizing the various services, interviewing and hiring store employees, dealing with distributors, and maintaining records of sales and animal health.

Kathryn Chambliss manages a small pet shop, The Fish Peddler, in Alabama. "This job is a natural outgrowth of my hobby," she says. "I have been breeding and showing dogs since I was a teenager. My children were always bringing home pets and injured animals for me to take care of, and I have always been very active in promoting responsible pet ownership and animal care issues." Both Kathryn and Max emphasize that working in a small pet shop is very different from working in the larger, discount, superstores. "We cannot match their prices," Kathryn says, "so we have to be better than they are in terms of service, friendliness, and working with the customer."

Requirements

For pet store work, you'll need to develop a good business sense, an ability to work well with customers, and a knowledge of animals and their care. In high school, accounting, marketing, and other business related courses are valuable, as are math courses. You'll need math for both money management and for figuring proper feed and medication amounts for the animals. The sciences are important for anyone working with animals. A knowledge of chemistry will come in handy when preparing medications and chemicals for the aquariums. Biology will introduce you to the biological systems of various kinds of animals. Geography courses can also add to your understanding of animals by introducing you to their natural habitats and origins.

A business club, such as Future Business Leaders of America, will introduce you to area business owners, and help you develop skills in advertising, marketing, and management. Agricultural clubs and 4-H clubs can teach you about animal care and responsibilities.

You can easily get work at a pet store without any college education or special training. As with most retail businesses, pet shops often employ high school students for part-time and summer positions. Store owners usually hire people with a love of animals, and some knowledge of their care, for entry-level positions such as clerk, cashier, and salesperson. For management positions, a pet shop owner may want someone with some higher education. It is also easier to advance into management positions if you have a college degree.

Though any college degree will be valuable for higher-level pet shop positions, you'll want to take courses in marketing, accounting, merchandising, and other business-related areas. Some pet shops also like to hire people with veterinary tech training. Students pursuing a pre-veterinary sciences degree often work part-time in a pet shop to gain experience with animals and their owners.

Because of the wide availability of retail work, you would be better advised to pursue a paid entry-level position at a store, rather than an internship. But belonging to a business organization as a student can offer you valuable insight into marketing and management. DECA, an association of marketing students, is an organization that prepares high school and junior college students for retail careers. There are many local chapters of DECA across the country, and annual leadership conferences. Some DECA chapters also offer scholarships to marketing students.

Though no certification is required for working in a pet shop, the Pet Industry Joint Advisory Council (PIJAC), the largest trade association in the pet industry, did recently introduce their Certified Animal Care Handler (ACH) program. The program offers pet shop workers seminars, workbooks, and exams in six subjects: avians, canines, felines, freshwater fish, reptiles, and small animals. Pet shop workers wanting to develop further animal care skills can talk to their employers about bringing the PIJAC program to their store.

"It takes a great deal of respect and love for animals," Max Paterson says about working in a pet shop, "a person who can help customers even when there are lots of them, and someone who's not afraid to get their hands dirty every now and again." As with any retail job, you must be prepared to serve people on a daily basis—you should be friendly and outgoing, and prepared to answer questions clearly and patiently. Though most of your encounters with these fellow animal-lovers will likely be pleasant, you must be prepared for the occasional dissatisfied customer; dealing with angry customers requires you to remain calm, and to settle the dispute diplomatically. You must remain informed on new products and animal care; customers will be asking you about the right size cages for particular birds, or how many fish a tank can hold. In answering such questions, your first concern must be for the well-being of the animals, not for the biggest profit. Some customers may even be testing you with their questions, making sure the store's staff is reliable. Kathryn Chambliss says, "I like just being around the animals, and people who like animals. I like helping people choose the right pet for their lifestyle. I like designing water gardens, and helping customers select the right mix of plant and fish for a beautiful addition to their home."

Depending on your duties at the pet store, you'll need analytical skills; you'll be analyzing data when ordering new products, choosing vendors, and examining sales figures and invoices. In whatever position you fill at the pet store, it will be important for you to manage your time well to deal with customers while keeping the store orderly and the shelves well-stocked.

Opportunities for Experience and Exploration

With the number of volunteer opportunities at animal shelters, zoos, and other animal care facilities, you can easily gain experience working with animals. You may also want to spend a few days "shadowing" some pet shop managers, following them throughout their work day to get a sense of their duties. Max Paterson, before going to work for the pet shop, spent a lot of his spare time there learning about the animals and the products for sale. "The first step was creating a trusting, customer/owner relationship," he says. "From there, I began asking if he needed some odd jobs done for a few bucks, and in doing these jobs, and just hanging out at the store, I began to pick up on all he was saying to the customers. Soon, I too knew enough to help customers."

Methods of Entering

After spending so much time at his local pet shop, and learning so much about the business, Max was able to step into a job. "I now work regular hours," he says, "and have often been left to watch the store on my own." Experience with animal care can help you get a job in a pet store, but such experience is not always required. A pet shop owner or manager may be prepared to give you on-the-job training. You can check the classified ads in your paper for pet shop jobs, but a better approach is to visit all the pet stores in your area and fill out applications. If you don't hear back from the store right away, follow up on a regular basis so that the manager or store owner gets to know you. That way, when there is a job opening, the manager will have you in mind.

For management positions, you should have some background in entry-level retail positions, and some college education. While pursuing that education, you can take part-time work in pet stores or other retail businesses. Though any retail experience is valuable, experience in a small pet store will involve you directly with many of the main concerns of a business; in a larger pet "megastore" your experience may be limited to a few duties.

Advancement

The longer you work in one store, the more responsibilities you're likely to be given. After starting as a cashier, or stock person, you may eventually be allowed to open and close the store, place orders, create advertisements, order new products, and deal with distributors. Experience in the many different areas of one particular business can lead to advancement from an entry-level position to a management position, even if you don't have a college education.

As a manager, you may be allowed to expand the store in new directions; with the understanding of a store and its clientele, you can introduce such additions as an animal training program, sponsorship of adopt-a-pet and animal-assisted therapy programs, and new product lines.

Employment Outlook

The larger pet stores, which can afford to offer special pricing, inexpensive grooming facilities, and free training programs, are taking much of the business away from the smaller, traditional, "mom and pop" pet shops. This trend is likely to continue, but small stores will survive as they promote a more personalized and knowledgeable assistance not available from the larger stores. The pet retail industry, in some form, will grow along with the retail industry in general; the U.S. Department of Labor predicts 24 million people will be employed in retail by the year 2005.

The puppies and kittens frolicking in the windows of corner pet shops are becoming a thing of the past as animal activists have made the public increasingly aware of "puppy mills" and other unregulated animal breeders. Groups such as the American Society for the Prevention of Cruelty to Animals (ASPCA) fight for better regulation of animal sales practices and animal care in pet shops.

Holistic pet care is also changing the industry—non-chemical remedies, natural foods, and vitamin supplements for animals are gaining more acceptance from store owners, animal breeders, and veterinarians. And, as with every industry, computers have influenced the way stores keep records of business, sales, and animal health. Pet shop managers will be expected to have some computer skills, and a basic understanding of bookkeeping software.

Earnings

"This is not a business that will ever make us rich," Kathryn points out. "Most of the time, the store generates enough in sales to pay bills, and very little else." Entry-level pet shop workers earn minimum wage, and even those with experience probably won't make much more than that. Though the average store manager makes under $30,000, there does seem to be the possibility of salary increases in the future. In order to attract more experienced store managers, store owners are beginning to reward managers for their varied responsibilities and extra hours. The size of the store also makes a difference; stores with larger volumes pay their managers considerably more than stores with volumes of less than one million dollars. The size of the store also determines the number of benefits for a full-time employee. In smaller stores, pet shop workers may not receive any health benefits or vacation pay, while a bigger store may have group health plans for managers.

Conditions of Work

A clean, healthy pet shop should make for a very comfortable work environment. But to keep the place clean and healthy, you'll be handling animals, cleaning out cages and fish tanks, and preparing medications. You'll also be sweeping the floors of the store, and dusting shelves. A pet shop should also be well-ventilated and temperature-controlled. During work hours, pet shop workers usually stay indoors and don't venture far from their assigned work stations.

Working in a public place devoted to the care of animals, some pet shop workers find themselves taking on extra responsibilities. "Every day," Kathryn says, " I have at least one person bring me an abused or uncared-for animal. I provide foster care for baby animals left at the Humane Society, and

I try to raise them, wean them, and find them homes. It is tragic that there is so little responsible pet ownership in this country." Though pet shop workers do their best to educate customers and to prepare them for pet ownership, they must still deal with fact that many animals in their community are without good homes.

Sources of Additional Information

For a brochure about entering retail careers, contact:

National Retail Federation
325 7th Street, NW, Suite 1000
Washington, DC 20004
Tel: 1-800-NRF-HOW2
WWW: http://www.nrf.com

For information about pet care, contact:

American Society for the Prevention of Cruelty to Animals
424 East 92nd Street
New York, NY 10128-6804
Tel: 212-876-7700
WWW: http://www.aspca.org

For information about their Certified Animal Care Handler program, contact:

Pet Industry Joint Advisory Council National Office
1220 19th Street, NW, Suite 400
Washington, DC 20036
WWW: http://petsforum.com/PIJAC

Pet Sitters

	School Subjects
Business	
Family and Consumer Science	

	Personal Interests
Animals	
Babysitting/Child care	
Helping people: personal service	

	Work Environment
Indoors and outdoors	
Primarily multiple locations	

	Minimum Education Level
High school diploma	

	Salary Range
$5,000 to $20,000 to $40,000	

	Certification or Licensing
Voluntary	

	Outlook
Faster than the average	

Definition

When pet owners are on vacation or working long hours, they hire *pet sitters* to come to their homes and visit their animals. During short, daily visits, pet sitters feed the animals, play with them, clean up after them, give them medications when needed, and let them in and out of the house for exercise. *Dog walkers* may be responsible only for taking their clients' pets out for exercise. Pet sitters may also be available for overnight stays, looking after the houses of clients as well as their pets.

History

Animals have been revered by humans for centuries, as is evidenced by early drawings on the walls of caves and tombs—cats were even considered sacred by the ancient Egyptians. Though these sacred cats may have had their own personal caretakers, it has only been within the last ten years that pet sitting has evolved into a successful industry and a viable career option. Before groups such as the National Association of Professional Pet Sitters (NAPPS), which formed in the early 1980s, and Pet Sitters International (PSI) were developed, pet sitting was regarded as a way for people with spare time to make a little extra money on the side. Like babysitting, pet sitting attracted primarily teenagers and women; many children's books over the last century have depicted the trials and tribulations of young entrepreneurs in the business of pet sitting and dog walking. Patti Moran, the founder of both NAPPS and PSI, and author of *Pet Sitting for Profit*, is credited with helping pet sitters gain recognition as successful small business owners. Though many people still only pet sit occasionally for neighbors and friends, others are developing long lists of clientele and proving strong competition to kennels and boarding facilities.

Nature of the Work

If you live in a big city, you've seen them hit the streets with their packs of dogs. Dragged along by four or five leashes, the pet sitter walks the dogs down the busy sidewalks, allowing the animals their afternoon exercise while the pet owners are stuck in the office. You may not have realized it, but those dog walkers are probably the owners of a thriving businesses. Though a hobby for some, pet sitting is for others a demanding career with many responsibilities. Michele Finley is one of these pet sitters, in the Park Slope neighborhood of Brooklyn, New York. "A lot of people seem to think pet sitting is a walk in the park (pun intended)," she says, "and go into it without realizing what it entails (again)."

For those who can't bear to leave their dogs or cats at kennels or boarders while they are away, pet sitters offer peace of mind to the owners, as well as their pets. With a pet sitter, pets can stay in familiar surroundings, as well as avoid the risks of illnesses passed on by other animals. The pets are also assured routine exercise and no disruptions in their diets. Most pet sitters prefer to work only with cats and dogs, but pet sitters are also called upon to care for birds, reptiles, gerbils, fish, and other animals.

With their own set of keys, pet sitters let themselves into the homes of their clients and care for their animals while they're away at work or on vacation. Pet sitters feed the animals, make sure they have water, and give them their medications. They clean up any messes the animals have made and clean litter boxes. They give the animals attention, playing with them, letting them outside, and taking them for walks. Usually, a pet sitter can provide pet owners with a variety of personal pet care services—they may take a pet to the vet, offer grooming, sell pet-related products, and give advice. Some pet sitters take dogs out into the country, to mountain parks, or to lakes, for exercise in wide-open spaces. "You should learn to handle each pet as an individual," Michele advises. "Just because Fluffy likes his ears scratched doesn't mean Spot does."

Pet sitters typically plan one to three visits (of thirty to sixty minutes in length) per day, or they may make arrangements to spend the night. In addition to caring for the animals, pet sitters also look after the houses of their clients. They bring in the newspapers and the mail; they water the plants; they make sure the house is securely locked. Pet sitters generally charge by the hour or per visit. They may also have special pricing for overtime, emergency situations, extra duties, and travel.

Most pet sitters work alone, without employees, no matter how demanding the work. Though this means getting to keep all the money, it also means keeping all the responsibilities. A successful pet sitting service requires a fair amount of business management. Michele works directly with the animals from 10:00 AM until 5:00 or 6:00 PM, with no breaks; upon returning home, she will have five to ten phone messages from clients. Part of her evening then consists of scheduling and rescheduling appointments, offering advice on feeding, training, and other pet care concerns, and giving referrals for boarders and vets. But despite these hours, and despite having to work holidays, as well as days when she's not feeling well, Michele appreciates many things about the job. "Being with the furries all day is the best," she says. She also likes not having to dress up for work and not having to commute to an office.

Requirements

As a pet sitter, you'll be running your own business all by yourself; therefore you should take high school courses such as accounting, marketing, and office skills. Computer science will help you learn about the software you'll need for managing accounts and scheduling. Join a school business group that will introduce you to business practices and local entrepreneurs.

Science courses such as biology and chemistry, as well as health courses, will give you some good background for developing animal care skills. As a pet sitter, you'll be overseeing the health of the animals, their exercise, and their diets. You'll also be preparing medications and administering eye and ear drops.

As a high school student, you can easily gain hands-on experience as a pet sitter. If you know anyone in your neighborhood with pets, volunteer to care for the animals whenever the owners go on vacation. Once you've got experience and a list of references, you may even be able to start a part-time job for yourself as a pet sitter.

Many pet sitters start their own businesses after having gained experience in other areas of animal care. Vet techs and pet shop workers may promote their animal care skills to develop a clientele for more profitable pet sitting careers. Graduates from a business college may recognize pet sitting as a great way to start a business with little overhead. But neither a vet tech qualification nor a business degree is required to become a successful pet sitter. And the only special training you need to pursue is actual experience. A local pet shop or chapter of the ASPCA may offer seminars in various aspects of animal care; the NAPPS offers a mentorship program, as well as a newsletter, while PSI sponsors correspondence programs. There are many publications devoted to pet care, such as *Dog Fancy* and *Cat Watch*, which can educate you about pet health and behavior.

PSI offers accreditation on four levels: *Pet Sitting Technician, Advanced Pet Sitting Technician, Master Professional Pet Sitter*, and Accredited Pet Sitting Service. Pet sitters receive accreditation upon completing home study courses in such subjects as animal nutrition, office procedures, and management. Because the accreditation program was developed only within the last few years, PSI estimates that less than 10 percent of pet sitters working today are accredited. That number is likely to increase, though there are no plans for any kind of government regulation that would require accreditation. "I really don't think such things are necessary," Michele says about accreditation. "All you need to know can be learned by working for a good sitter and reading pet health and behavioral newsletters."

Though there is no particular pet-sitting license required of pet sitters, insurance protection is important. Liability insurance protects the pet sitter from lawsuits; both NAPPS and PSI offer group liability packages to its members. Pet sitters must also be bonded. Bonding assures the pet owners that if anything is missing from their homes after a pet sitting appointment, they can receive compensation immediately.

You must love animals and animals must love you. But this love for animals can't be your only motivation—keep in mind that, as a pet sitter, you'll be in business for yourself. You won't have a boss to give you assignments, and you won't have a secretary or bookkeeper to do the paperwork. You also won't have employees to take over on weekends, holidays, and days when you're not feeling well. Though some pet sitters are successful enough to afford assistance, most must handle all the aspects of their businesses by themselves. So, you should be self-motivated, and as dedicated to the management of your business as you are to the animals.

Pet owners are entrusting you with the care of their pets and their homes, so you must be trustworthy and reliable. You should also be organized and prepared for emergency situations. And not only must you be patient with the pets and their owners, but also with the development of your business: it will take a few years to build up a good list of clients.

As a pet sitter, you must also be ready for the dirty work—you'll be cleaning litter boxes and animal messes within the house. On dog walks, you'll be picking up after them on the street. You may be giving animals medications. You'll also be cleaning aquariums and bird cages.

"Work for an established pet sitter to see how you like it," Michele advises. "It's a very physically demanding job and not many can stand it for long on a full-time basis." Pet sitting isn't for those who just want a nine-to-five desk job. Your day will be spent moving from house to house, taking animals into backyards, and walking dogs around the neighborhoods. Though you may be able to develop a set schedule for yourself, you really will have to arrange your work hours around the hours of your clients. Some pet sitters start in the early morning hours, while others only work afternoons or evenings. To stay in business, a pet sitter must be prepared to work weekends, holidays, and long hours in the summer time.

Opportunities for Experience and Exploration

There are many books, newsletters, and magazines devoted to pet care. *Pet Sitting for Profit*, by Patti Moran, and *The Professional Pet Sitter* by Lori and Scott Mangold, are a few of the books that can offer insight into pet sitting as a career. Magazines such as *Cat Fancy* can also teach you about the requirements of animal care. And there are any number of books discussing the ins and outs of small business ownership.

Try pet sitting for a neighbor or family member to get a sense of the responsibilities of the job. Some pet sitters hire assistants on an independent contractor basis; contact an area pet sitter listed in the phone book or with one of the professional organizations, and see if you can "hire on" for a day or two. Not only will you learn first-hand the duties of a pet sitter, but you'll also see how the business is run.

Methods of Entering

You're not likely to find job listings under "pet sitter" in the newspaper. Most pet sitters schedule all their work themselves. However, you may find ads in the classifieds or in weekly community papers, from pet owners looking to hire pet sitters. Some people who become pet sitters have backgrounds in animal care—they may have worked for vets, breeders, or pet shops. These people enter the business with a client list already in hand, having made contacts with many pet owners. But, if you're just starting out in animal care, you need to develop a list of references. This may mean volunteering your time to friends and neighbors, or working very cheaply. If you're willing to actually stay in the house while the pet owners are on vacation, you should be able to find plenty of pet sitting opportunities in the summertime. Post your name, phone number, and availability on the bulletin boards of grocery stores, colleges, and coffee shops around town. Once you've developed a list of references, and have made connections with pet owners, you can start expanding, and increasing your profits.

Advancement

Your advancement will be a result of your own hard work; the more time you dedicate to your business, the bigger the business will become. The success of any small business can be very unpredictable. For some, a business can build very quickly, for others it may take years. Some pet sitters start out part-time, perhaps even volunteering, then may find themselves with enough business to quit their full-time jobs and to devote themselves entirely to pet sitting. Once your business takes off, you may be able to afford an assistant, or an entire staff. Some pet sitters even have franchises across the country. You may even choose to develop your business into a much larger operation, such as a dog day care facility.

Employment Outlook

Pet sitting as a small business is expected to skyrocket in the coming years. Most pet sitters charge fees comparable to kennels and boarders, but some charge less. And many pet owners prefer to leave their pets in the house, rather than take the pets to unfamiliar locations. This has all made pet sitting a desirable and cost-effective alternative to other pet care situations. Pet sitters have been successful in cities both large and small. In the last few years, pet sitting has been featured in the *Wall Street Journal* and other national publications; last year, *Woman's Day* magazine listed pet sitting as one of the top-grossing businesses for women. Pet Sitters International has grown 500 percent in the last four years.

Because a pet sitting business requires little money to start up, many more people may enter the business hoping to make a tidy profit. This could lead to heavier competition; it could also hurt the reputation of pet sitting if too many irresponsible and unprepared people run bad businesses. But if pet owners remain cautious when hiring pet sitters, the unreliable workers will have trouble maintaining clients.

Earnings

Pet sitters set their own prices, charging by the visit, the hour, or the week. They may also charge consultation fees, and additional fees on holidays. They may have special pricing plans in place, such as for emergency situations or for administering medications. Depending on the kinds of animals (sometimes pet sitters charge less to care for cats than dogs), pet sitters generally charge between $8 and $15 a visit (with a visit lasting between thirty and sixty minutes). PSI conducted a recent salary survey and discovered that the range was too great to determine a median. Some very successful pet sitters have annual salaries of over $100,000, while others only make $5,000 a year. Though a pet sitter can make a good profit in any area of the country, a bigger city will offer more clients. Pet sitters in their first five years of business are unlikely to make more than $10,000 a year; pet sitters who have had businesses for eight years or more may make more than $40,000 a year.

Conditions of Work

Some pet sitters prefer to work close to their homes; Michele only walks dogs in her Brooklyn neighborhood. In a smaller town, however, pet sitters have to do a fair amount of driving from place to place. Depending on the needs of the animals, the pet sitter will let the pets outside for play and exercise. Although filling food and water bowls and performing other chores within the house is generally peaceful work, walking dogs on the busy city sidewalks can be stressful. And in the winter time, you'll spend a fair amount of time out in the inclement weather. "Icy streets are murder," Michele says. "And I don't like dealing with people who hate dogs and are always yelling to the get the dog away from them."

Though you'll have some initial interaction with pet owners when getting house keys, taking down phone numbers, and meeting the pets and learning about their needs, most of your work will be alone with the animals. But you won't be totally isolated; if dog walking in the city, you'll meet other dog owners and other people in the neighborhood.

Sources of Additional Information

For career and small business information, as well as general information about pet sitting, contact these organizations:

Pet Sitters International
418 East King Street
King, NC 27021-9163
Tel: 336-983-9222
WWW: http://www.petsit.com

National Association of Professional Pet Sitters
1200 G Street, NW, Suite 760
Washington, DC 20005
Tel: 202-393-3317
WWW: http://www.petsitters.com

Veterinarians

Anatomy and Physiology Biology	School Subjects
Animals Science Wildlife	Personal Interests
Primarily indoors Primarily one location	Work Environment
Medical degree	Minimum Education Level
$29,900 to $44,500 to $57,600	Salary Range
Required	Certification or Licensing
Faster than the average	Outlook

Definition

The *veterinarian*, or *doctor of veterinary medicine*, diagnoses and controls animal diseases, treats sick and injured animals medically and surgically, prevents transmission of animal diseases, and advises owners on proper care of pets and livestock. Veterinarians are dedicated to the protection of the health and welfare of all animals and to society as a whole.

History

The first school of veterinary medicine was opened in 1762 at Lyons, France and it was a French immigrant who established the practice of veterinary medicine in the United States one hundred years later. Veterinary medicine has made great strides since its introduction in this country, one advance being the significant reduction in animal diseases contracted by humans.

Nature of the Work

Veterinarians ensure a safe food supply by maintaining the health of food animals. They also protect the public from residues of herbicides, pesticides, and antibiotics in food. Veterinarians may be involved in wildlife preservation and conservation, and use their knowledge to increase food production through genetics, animal feed production, and preventive medicine.

In North America, about 80 percent of veterinarians are in private clinical practice. Although some veterinarians treat all kinds of animals, about half limit their practice to companion animals such as dogs, cats, and birds. Of the veterinarians in private practice, about 11 percent work mainly with horses, cattle, pigs, sheep, goats, and poultry. Today, a veterinarian may be treating llamas, catfish, or ostriches as well. Others are employed by wildlife management groups, zoos, aquariums, ranches, feed lots, fish farms, and animal shelters.

The remaining 20 percent of veterinarians work in public and corporate sectors. Many veterinarians are employed by city, county, state, provincial, or federal governmental agencies that investigate, test for, and control diseases in companion animals, livestock, and poultry that affect both animal and human health.

Veterinarians are utilized by pharmaceutical and biomedical research firms to develop, test, and supervise the production of drugs, chemicals, and biological products such as antibiotics and vaccines that are designed for human and animal use. Some veterinarians are employed in management, technical sales and services, and marketing in agribusiness, pet food companies, and pharmaceutical companies. Still other veterinarians are engaged in research and teaching at veterinary and human medical schools, working with racetracks or animal-related enterprises, or work within the military, public health corps, and space agencies.

Other veterinarians in private clinical practice become specialists in surgery, anesthesiology, dentistry, internal medicine, ophthalmology, or radiology. Many veterinarians also pursue advanced degrees in the basic sciences such as anatomy, microbiology, and physiology. Veterinarians who seek specialty board certification in one of twenty specialty fields must complete a two- to five-year residency program and must pass an additional examination. Some veterinarians combine their degree in veterinary medicine with a degree in business (MBA) or law (JD).

Veterinarians are employed in various branches of federal, state, provincial, county, or city government. The U.S. Department of Agriculture has opportunities for veterinarians in the food safety inspection service and the animal and plant health inspection service, notably in the areas of food hygiene and safety, animal welfare, animal disease control, and research.

Agencies in the U.S. Department of Agriculture utilize veterinarians in positions related to research on diseases transmissible from animal to human beings and on acceptance and the use of drugs for treatment or prevention of diseases. Veterinarians also are employed by the Environmental Protection Agency to deal with public health and environmental risks to the human population.

Requirements

All states and the District of Columbia require that veterinarians be licensed to practice private clinical medicine. To obtain a license, applicants must have a doctor of veterinary medicine (D.V.M.) degree from an accredited or approved college of veterinary medicine. They must also pass one or more national examinations and an examination in the state in which they are applying.

A veterinarian does not have to complete an internship in order to practice clinical medicine. Some states issue licenses without further examination to veterinarians already licensed by another state. Approximately half of the states require veterinarians to attend continuing education courses in order to maintain their licenses. Veterinarians may be employed by a government agency (such as the U.S. Department of Agriculture) or at some academic institution without having a state license. For positions in research and teaching, a master's degree or Ph.D. is usually required.

The D.V.M. degree requires a minimum of six years of college after graduation from high school, consisting of at least two years of preveterinary study that emphasizes physical and biological sciences and a four-year veterinary program. It is possible to obtain preveterinary training in a junior college. Most preveterinary students, however, enroll in four-year colleges. In addition to academic instruction, veterinary education includes clinical experience in diagnosing disease and treating animals, performing surgery, and performing laboratory work in anatomy, biochemistry, and other scientific and medical subjects.

In 1997, all twenty-seven colleges of veterinary medicine in the United States were accredited by the Council of Veterinary Medicine of the American Veterinary Medical Association (AVMA). Each college of veterinary medicine has its own preveterinary requirements, which typically include basic language arts, social sciences, humanities, mathematics, chemistry, and the biological and physical sciences.

Admission to schools of veterinary medicine is highly competitive. Applicants usually must have grades of "B" or better, especially in the sciences. Applicants must take the Veterinary Aptitude Test, Medical College Admission Test, or the Graduate Record Examination. Fewer than half of the applicants to schools of veterinary medicine may be admitted, due to small class sizes and limited facilities. Most colleges give preference to candidates with animal- or veterinary-related experience. Colleges usually give preference to in-state applicants because most colleges of veterinary medicine are state-supported. There are regional agreements in which states without veterinary schools send students to designated regional schools. For the high school student who is interested in admission to a school of veterinary medicine, a college-preparatory course with a strong emphasis on science is a wise choice.

Individuals who are interested in veterinary medicine should have an enquiring mind and keen powers of observation. Aptitude and interest in the biological sciences are important. Veterinarians need a lifelong interest in scientific learning as well as a liking and understanding of animals. Veterinarians should be able to meet, talk, and work well with a variety of people. An ability to communicate with the animal owner is as important in a veterinarian as diagnostic skills.

Veterinarians use state-of-the-art medical equipment, such as electron microscopes, laser surgery, radiation therapy, and ultrasound, to diagnose animal diseases and to treat sick or injured animals. Although manual dexterity and physical stamina are often required, especially for farm vets, important roles in veterinary medicine can be adapted for those with disabilities.

Veterinarians may have to euthanize (that is, humanely kill) an animal that is very sick or severely injured and cannot get well. When an animal such as a beloved pet dies, the veterinarian must deal with the owner's grief and loss.

Opportunities for Experience and Exploration

High school students interested in becoming veterinarians may find part-time or volunteer work on farms, in small-animal clinics, pet shops, animal shelters, or research laboratories. Participation in extracurricular activities such as 4-H are good ways to learn about the care of animals. Such experience is important because, as already noted, many schools of veterinary medicine have established experience with animals as a criterion for admission to their programs.

Methods of Entering

The only way to become a veterinarian is through the prescribed degree program, and vet schools are set up to assist their graduates in finding employment. Veterinarians who wish to enter private clinical practice must have a license to practice in their particular state before opening an office. Licenses are obtained by passing the state's examination.

Advancement

New graduate veterinarians may enter private clinical practice, usually as employees in an established practice, or become employees of the U.S. government as meat and poultry inspectors, disease control workers, and commissioned officers in the U.S. Public Health Service or the military. New graduates may also enter internships and residencies at veterinary colleges and large private and public veterinary practices or become employed by industrial firms.

The veterinarian who is employed by a government agency may advance in grade and salary after accumulating time and experience on the job. For the veterinarian in private clinical practice, advancement usually consists of an expanding practice and the higher income that will result from it or becoming an owner of several practices.

Those who teach or do research may obtain a doctorate and move from the rank of instructor to that of full professor, or advance to an administrative position.

Employment Outlook

In 1996, about 70 percent of the more than 58,000 veterinarians were employed in private clinical practice. The federal government employed about 2,000, mostly in the Department of Agriculture and the Public Health

Service. The remainder were employees of private clinical practices, industry, or schools and universities.

Employment of veterinarians is expected to grow faster then the average through the year 2006. The number of pets is expected to increase slightly because of the rising incomes and an increase in the number of people in the thirty-four- to fifty-nine-year age group, where pet ownership has been highest in the past. Single adults and senior citizens have come to appreciate animal ownership. Pet owners also may be willing to pay for more elective and intensive care than in the past. In addition, emphasis on scientific methods of breeding and raising livestock, poultry, and fish and continued support for public health and disease control programs will contribute to the demand for veterinarians. The number of jobs stemming from the need to replace workers will be equal to new job growth.

The outlook is good for veterinarians with specialty training. Demand for specialists in toxicology, laboratory animal medicine, and pathology is expected to increase. Most jobs for specialists will be in metropolitan areas. Prospects for veterinarians who concentrate on environmental and public health issues, aquaculture, and food animal practice appear to be excellent because of perceived increased need in these areas. Positions in small animal specialties will be competitive. Opportunities in large animal specialties will be better since most such positions are located in remote, rural areas.

Despite the availability of additional jobs, competition among veterinarians is likely to be stiff. First-year enrollments in veterinary schools have increased slightly and the number of students in graduate-degree and board-certification programs has risen dramatically.

Earnings

According to the American Veterinary Medical Association, newly graduated veterinarians employed by the federal government start at salaries of about $35,800 a year. The average yearly salary of veterinarians working for the federal government is about $57,600. For those in industry, the average yearly salary for veterinarians is about $44,500.

The earnings of veterinarians in private clinical practice varies according to practice location, type of practice, and years of experience. New graduates employed in the established private clinical practices of other veterinarians generally are paid an average of $29,900 a year. The average income of veterinarians in private clinical practice was $57,500 in 1995. Owners of private clinical practices must operate their practices as a small business. The average starting income for practice owners specializing in large animal care was $39,500 compared with an average income of $31,900 for veterinarians specializing in small animal care.

Conditions of Work

Veterinarians usually treat companion and food animals in hospitals and clinics. Those in large animal practice also work out of well-equipped trucks or cars and may drive considerable distances to farms and ranches. They may work outdoors in all kinds of weather. The chief risk for veterinarians is injury by animals; however, modern tranquilizers and technology have made it much easier to work on all types of animals.

Most veterinarians work fifty or more hours per week; however, about a fifth work forty hours per week. Although those in private clinical practice may work nights and weekends, the increased number of emergency clinics has reduced the amount of time private practitioners have to be on call. Large animal practitioners tend to work more irregular hours than those in small animal practice, industry, or government. Veterinarians who are just starting a practice tend to work longer hours.

Sources of Additional Information

For more information on veterinary careers and how to prepare for them, get in touch with the following organizations:

American Veterinary Medical Association
1931 North Meacham Road, Suite 100
Schaumburg, IL 60173-4360
Tel: 800-248-2862 or 847-925-8070
WWW: http://www.avma.org

U.S. Department of Agriculture
Animal and Plant Health Inspection Service
Butler Square West, 4th Floor
100 North Sixth Street
Minneapolis, MN 55403

Veterinary Technicians

Biology
Science
———————————————————School Subjects

Animals
Science
Wildlife
———————————————————Personal Interests

Primarily indoors
Primarily one location
———————————————————Work Environment

Associate's degree
———————————————————Minimum Education Level

$15,000 to $40,000
———————————————————Salary Range

Required by certain states
———————————————————Certification or Licensing

Faster than the average
———————————————————Outlook

Definition

Veterinary technicians are professionals who provide support and assistance to veterinary doctors. They work in a variety of environments, including zoos, animal hospitals, clinics, private practices, kennels, and laboratories. Work may involve large or small animals, or both. Although most veterinary technicians work with domestic animals, some professional settings may require treating exotic or endangered species.

History

As the scope of veterinary practices grew and developed, veterinarians began to require assistants. At first the role was informal, with veterinary assistants being trained by the D.V.M.s they worked for. In the latter half of this century, however, the education--and thus the profession--of veterinary assistants became formalized

Nature of the Work

Many pet owners depend upon veterinarians to maintain the health and well-being of their pets. Veterinary clinics and private practices are the primary settings for animal care. In assisting veterinarians, veterinary technicians play an integral role in the care of animals within this particular environment.

A veterinary technician is the person who performs much of the laboratory testing procedures commonly associated with veterinary care. In fact, approximately 50 percent of a veterinary technician's duties involves laboratory testing. Laboratory assignments usually include taking and developing x-rays, performing parasitology tests, and examining various samples taken from the animal's body, such as blood and stool. A veterinary technician may also assist the veterinarian with necropsies in an effort to determine the cause of an animal's death.

In a clinic or private practice, a veterinary technician assists the veterinarian with surgical procedures. This generally entails preparing the animal for surgery by shaving the incision area and applying a topical antibacterial agent. Surgical anesthesia is administered and controlled by the veterinary technician. Throughout the surgical process, the technician tracks the surgical instruments and monitors the animal's vital signs. If an animal is very ill and has no chance for survival or an overcrowded animal shelter is unable to find a home for a donated or stray animal, the veterinary technician may be required to assist in euthanizing it.

During routine examinations and check ups, veterinary technicians will help restrain the animals. They may perform ear cleaning and nail clipping procedures as part of regular animal care. Outside the examination and surgery rooms, veterinary technicians perform additional duties. In most settings, they record, replenish, and maintain pharmaceutical equipment and other supplies.

Veterinary technicians may also work in a zoo. Here, job duties, such as laboratory testing, are quite similar, but practices are more specialized. Unlike in private practice, the *zoo veterinary technician* is not required to explain treatment to pet owners; however, he or she may have to discuss an animal's treatment or progress with *zoo veterinarians*, *zoo curators*, and other zoo professionals. A zoo veterinary technician's work may also differ from private practice in that it may be necessary for the technician to observe the animal in its habitat, which could require working outdoors. Additionally, zoo veterinary technicians usually work with exotic or endangered species. This is a very competitive and highly desired area of practice in the veterinary technician field. Currently there are only fifty zoo veterinary technicians working in the United States. There are only a few zoos in each state; thus a limited number of job opportunities exist within these zoos. To break into this area of practice, veterinary technicians must be among the best in the field.

Another setting where veterinary technicians work is research. Most research opportunities for veterinary technicians are in academic environments with veterinary medicine or medical science programs. Again, laboratory testing may account for many of the duties; however, the veterinary technicians participate in very important animal research projects from start to finish.

Technicians are also needed in rural areas. Farmers require veterinary services for the care of farm animals such as pigs, cows, horses, dogs, cats, sheep, mules, and chickens. It is often essential for the veterinarian and technician to drive to the farmer's residence because animals are usually treated on site.

Another area in which veterinary technicians work is that of animal training, such as at an obedience school or with show business animals being trained for the circus or movies. Veterinary technicians may also be employed in information systems technology, where information on animals is compiled and provided to the public via the Internet.

No matter what the setting, a veterinary technician must be an effective communicator and proficient in basic computer applications. In clinical or private practice, it is usually the veterinary technician who conveys and explains treatment and subsequent animal care to the animal's owner. In research and laboratory work, the veterinary technician must record and discuss results among colleagues. In most practical veterinary settings, the veterinary technician must record various information on a computer.

Requirements

A high school diploma is necessary in order to obtain the required training. High school students who excel at math and science have a strong foundation on which to build. Those who have had pets or who simply love animals and would like to work with them also fit the profile of a veterinary technician.

The main requirement is the completion of a two- to four-year college-based accredited program. Upon graduation, the student receives an associate's or bachelor's degree. Currently, there are sixty-five accredited programs in the United States. A few states do their own accrediting, using the American Veterinary Medical Association (AVMA) and associated programs as benchmarks.

Most accredited programs offer thorough course work and preparatory learning opportunities to the aspiring veterinary technician. Typical courses include mathematics, chemistry, humanities, biological science, communications, microbiology, liberal arts, ethics/jurisprudence, and basic computers.

Once the students complete this framework, they move on to more specialized courses. Students take advanced classes in animal nutrition, animal care and management, species/breed identification, veterinary anatomy/physiology, medical terminology, radiography and other clinical procedure courses, animal husbandry, parasitology, laboratory animal care, and large/small animal nursing.

Veterinary technicians must be prepared to assist in surgical procedures. In consideration of this, accredited programs offer surgical nursing courses. In these courses, a student learns to identify and use surgical instruments, administer anesthesia, and monitor the animal during and after surgery.

In addition to classroom study, accredited programs offer practical courses. Hands-on education and training are commonly achieved through a clinical practicum, or internship, where the student has the opportunity to work in a clinical veterinary setting. During this period, a student is continuously evaluated by the participating veterinarian and encouraged to apply the knowledge and skills learned.

Although the AVMA determines the majority of the national codes for veterinary technicians, state codes and laws vary. Most states offer registration or certification, and the majority of these states require graduation from an AVMA-accredited program as a prerequisite for taking the examination. Most colleges and universities assist graduates with registration and certification arrangements. To keep abreast of new technology and applications in the field, practicing veterinary technicians may be required to complete a determined amount of annual continuing education courses.

Opportunities for Experience and Exploration

High school students can acquire exposure to the veterinary field by working with animals in related settings. For example, a high school student may be able to work as a part-time animal attendant or receptionist in a private veterinary practice. Paid or volunteer positions may be available at kennels, animal shelters, and training schools. However, direct work with animals in a zoo is unlikely for high school students.

Methods of Entering

Veterinary technicians who complete an accredited program and become certified or registered by the state in which they plan to practice are often able to receive assistance in finding a job through their college placement offices. Students who have completed internships may receive job offers from the place where they interned

Veterinary technician graduates may also learn of clinic openings through classified ads in newspapers. Opportunities in zoos and research are usually listed in specific industry periodicals such as *Veterinary Technician Magazine* and *AZVT News*, a newsletter published by the Association of Zoo Veterinary Technicians.

Advancement

Where a career as a veterinary technician leads is entirely up to the individual. Opportunities are unlimited. With continued education, veterinary technicians can move into allied fields such as veterinary medicine, nursing, medical technology, radiology, and pharmacology. By completing two more years of college and receiving a bachelor's degree, a veterinary technician can become a *veterinary technologist*. Advanced degrees can open the doors to a variety of specialized fields. There are currently efforts to standardize requirements for veterinary technicians. A national standard would broaden the scope of educational programs and may create more opportunities in instruction for veterinary professionals with advanced degrees.

Employment Outlook

The employment outlook for veterinary technicians is very good through the year 2006. Veterinary technicians are constantly in demand. Veterinary medicine is a field that is not adversely affected by the economy, so it does offer stability.

In 1996, there were 33,000 veterinary technicians employed in the United States. Currently, there is a shortage of veterinary technicians. In fact, there were 4,000 job openings for every 1,000 graduates in the mid-1990's.

The public's love for pets coupled with higher disposable incomes will raise the demand for this occupation.

Earnings

Earnings are generally low for veterinary technicians in private practices and clinics, but pay scales are steadily climbing due to the increasing demand. Better-paying jobs are in zoos and in research. Those fields of practice are very competitive, especially zoos, and only a small percentage of highly qualified veterinary technicians are employed in them.

About 70 percent of veterinary technicians are employed in private or clinical practice and research. Earnings for zoo veterinary technicians range from $17,000 to $35,000. Salaries in clinical or private practice range from $15,000 for recent graduates to $40,000 for experienced graduates working in supervisory positions. Earnings vary depending on practice setting, geographic location, level of education, and years of experience. Benefits vary and depend on each employer's policies.

Conditions of Work

Veterinary technicians generally work forty-hour weeks, which may include a few long weekdays and alternated or rotated Saturdays. Hours may fluctuate as veterinary technicians may need to have their schedules adjusted to accommodate emergency work.

A veterinary technician must be prepared for emergencies. In field or farm work, they often have to overcome weather conditions in treating the animal. Injured animals can be very dangerous, and veterinary technicians have to exercise extreme caution when caring for them. A veterinary technician also handles animals that are diseased or infested with parasites. Some of these conditions, such as ringworm, are contagious, so the veterinary technician must understand how these conditions are transferred to humans and the measures needed to prevent the spread of diseases.

People who become veterinary technicians care about animals. For this reason, maintaining an animal's well-being or helping to cure an ill animal is very rewarding work. In private practice, technicians get to know the animals they care for. This provides the opportunity to actually see the animals' progress. In other areas, such as zoo work, veterinary technicians work with very interesting, sometimes endangered, species. This work can be challenging and rewarding in the sense that they are helping to save a species and continuing efforts to educate people about these animals. Veterinary technicians who work in research gain satisfaction from knowing their work contributes to promoting both animal and human health.

Sources of Additional Information

For more information on careers and resources, write to the American Veterinary Medical Association. In addition, check out the AVMA's Web page for career and education information, especially the "NetVet" link that provides access to information on specialties, organizations, publications, and fun sites.

American Veterinary Medical Association
1931 North Meacham Road, Suite 100
Schaumburg, IL 60173-4360
Tel: 800-248-2862 or 847-925-8070
WWW: http://www.avma.org

North American Veterinary Technician Association
PO Box 224
Battleground, IN 47920
Tel: 317-742-2216

Canadian Veterinary Medical Association
339 Booth Street
Ottawa, Ontario K1R 7K1 Canada
Tel: 613-236-1162
Email: mmcvma@magi.com

For more information on zoo veterinary technology and positions, contact:

Association of Zoo Veterinary Technicians
c/o Louisville Zoo
AZVT Office
PO Box 37250
Louisville, KY 40233
Tel: 502-451-0440

Zoo and Aquarium Curators

School Subjects
Biology
Business
Computer science
English (writing/literature)
Speech

Personal Interests
Animals
Business
Business management
The Environment
Wildlife

Work Environment
Indoors and outdoors
Primarily one location

Minimum Education Level
Bachelor's degree

Salary Range
$20,000 to $40,000 to $79,000

Certification or Licensing
None

Outlook
Little change or more slowly than
the average

DOT
102

GOE
11.02.01

NOC
0212

Definition

Zoos are wild kingdoms, and aquariums are underwater worlds. The word zoo comes from the Greek for "living being" and is a shortened term for zoological garden or zoological park; although this may imply that zoos are created just for beauty and recreation, the main functions of modern zoos are education, conservation, and the study of animals. The term aquarium comes from the Latin for "source of water"; in such places, living aquatic plants and animals are studied and exhibited. These land and water gardens are tended by people with an affinity for animals. *Curators* at zoos and aquariums are the chief employees responsible for the care of the creatures found at these public places; they oversee the various sections of the animal collections, such as birds, mammals, and fishes.

History

Prehistoric humans did not try to tame animals; for purposes of survival, they hunted them to avoid danger as well as to obtain food. The full history of the establishment of zoos and aquariums can be traced probably as far back as the earliest attempts by humans to domesticate animals after realizing that they could live with them as fellow creatures. The precise timing of this phenomenon is not known; it apparently occurred at different times in different parts of the world.

Ancient Sumerians kept fish in man-made ponds around 4,500 years ago. By 1150 BC, pigeons, elephants, antelope, and deer were held captive for taming in such areas as the Middle East, India, and China. In 1000 BC, a Chinese emperor named Wen Wang built a zoo and called it the Garden of Intelligence. Also around this time, the Chinese and Japanese were breeding and raising goldfish and carp for their beauty.

Zoos were abundant in ancient Greece; animals were held in captivity for purposes of study in nearly every city-state. In early Egypt and Asia, zoos were created mainly for public show, and during the Roman Empire, fish were kept in ponds and animals were collected both for arena showings and for private zoos. A fantastic zoo, with three hundred keepers taking care of birds, mammals, and reptiles, was created in Mexico in the early sixteenth century by Hernando Cortes (1485-1547), the Spanish conqueror.

Zoo and aquarium professions as we know them today began to be established around the mid-eighteenth century with the construction of various extravagant European zoos. The Imperial Menagerie of the Schönbrunn Zoo in Vienna, Austria, was opened in 1765 and still operates to this day. One of the most significant openings occurred in 1828 at the London Zoological Society's Regent's Park. The London Zoo continues to have one of the world's most extensive and popular collection of animals, with more than 8,900 examples of 1,200 species, including some of the rarest animals. The world's first public aquarium was also established at Regent's Park, in 1853, after which aquariums were built in other European cities. In the United

States, P. T. Barnum (1810-1891) was the first to establish a display aquarium, which opened in New York in 1856.

Of the aquariums located in most large cities throughout the world, the largest research facilities include the Oceanographic Institute (Monaco) and the Scripps Institution of Oceanography (California). Commercial aquariums include Sea World of California and the Seaquarium (Florida), which show fish in tanks that hold as much as one million gallons of water. Among the more than one thousand zoos worldwide, San Diego's nineteen hundred-acre Zoological Garden and Wild Animal Park has the world's largest animal collection. Its design is unique, with high mesas, steep canyons, and exotic landscaping that are a natural fit for many of its animal species.

Today, curators have a host of responsibilities involved with the operation of zoos and aquariums. Although many zoos and aquariums are separate places, there are also zoos that contain aquariums as part of their facilities. There are both public and private institutions, large and small, and curators often contribute their knowledge to the most effective methods of design, maintenance, and administration for these institutions.

Nature of the Work

General curators of zoos and aquariums oversee the management of an institution's entire animal collection and animal management staff. They help the *director* coordinate activities, such as education, collection planning, exhibit design, new construction, research, and public services. They meet with the director and other members of the staff to create long term strategic plans. General curators may have public relations and development responsibilities, such as meeting with the media and identifying and cultivating donors. In most institutions, general curators develop policy; other curators implement policy.

Animal curators are responsible for the day-to-day management of a specific portion of a zoo's or aquarium's animal collection (as defined taxonomically, such as mammals or birds, or ecogeographically, such as the Forest Edge or the Arizona Trail); the people charged with caring for that collection, including *assistant curators*, *zookeepers*, administrative staff such as secretaries, as well as researchers, students, and volunteers; and the associated facilities and equipment.

For example, the curator in charge of the mammal department of a large zoo would be responsible for the care of such animals as lions, tigers, monkeys, and elephants. He or she might oversee nearly a thousand animals, representing about two hundred different species, and scores of employees and have a multimillion dollar budget.

Assistant curators report to curators and assist in animal management tasks and decisions. They may have extensive supervisory responsibilities.

Curators have diverse responsibilities and their activities vary widely from day to day. They oversee animal husbandry procedures, including the daily care of the animals, establish proper nutritional programs, and manage animal health delivery in partnership with the veterinary staff. They develop exhibits, educational programs, and visitor services and participate in research and conservation activities. They maintain inventories of animals and other records, and they recommend and implement acquisitions and dispositions of animals. Curators serve as liaisons with other departments.

Curators prepare budgets and reports. They interview and hire new workers. When scientific conferences are held, curators attend them as representatives of the institutions for which they work. They are often called upon to write articles for scientific journals and perhaps provide information for newspaper reports and magazine stories. They may coordinate or participate in on site research or conservation efforts. To keep abreast with developments in their field, curators spend a lot of time reading.

Curators meet with the general curator, the director, and other staff to develop the objectives and philosophy of the institution and decide on the best way to care for and exhibit the animals. They must be knowledgeable about the animals' housing requirements, daily care, medical procedures, dietary needs, and social and reproduction habits. Curators represent their zoo or aquarium in collaborative efforts with other institutions, such as the more than eighty AZA Species Survival Plans that target individual species for intense conservation efforts by zoos and aquariums. In this capacity, curators may exchange information, negotiate breeding loans, or assemble the necessary permits and paperwork to effect the transfers. Other methods of animal acquisition coordinated by curators involve purchases from animal dealers or private collectors and collection of nonendangered species from the wild. Curators may arrange for the quarantine of newly acquired animals. They may arrange to send the remains of dead animals to museums or universities for study.

Curators often work on special projects. They may serve on multidisciplinary committees responsible for planning and constructing new exhibits. Curators interface with colleagues from other states and around the world in collaborative conservation efforts.

Although most zoo and aquarium curators check on the collection on a regular basis, they are usually more involved with administrative issues than animal husbandry. Much of their time is spent in meetings or writing email or on talking on the phone. "I value the times I get out to do rounds," said Mike Mulligan, Curator of Fishes at the John G. Shedd Aquarium in Chicago,

Illinois. "It's amazing what you miss if you're not out there every day. You see snapshots rather than the natural progression. But the best part of my job is being involved in planning the future of the Aquarium. It's very challenging and rewarding to be a player on the institutional level."

In addition to animal curators, large institutions employ curators whose responsibilities involve areas other than animal husbandry, such as research, conservation, exhibits, horticulture, and education.

Requirements

High school students who want to prepare for careers in upper management in zoos and aquariums should take classes in the sciences, especially biology, microbiology, chemistry, and physics, as well as in mathematics, computer sciences, language, and speech.

Reading about animals or surfing the Internet; taking classes at local zoos and aquariums; or joining clubs, such as 4-H or Audubon, can help students learn about animals. Taking time to learn about ecology and nature in general will prepare students for the systems-oriented approach used by modern zoo and aquarium managers. "Tomorrow's curators need to develop an understanding of the complexity and interconnectedness of wild things and wild places," said Dennis Pate, senior vice president and general curator of Chicago's Lincoln Park Zoo.

Volunteering at zoos or aquariums, animal shelters, wildlife rehabilitation facilities, stables, or veterinary hospitals demonstrates a serious commitment to animals and provides first-hand experience with them.

Professional organizations, such as the American Zoo and Aquarium Association (AZA) and the American Association of Zoo Keepers, Inc. (AAZK), have special membership rates for nonprofessionals. Associate members receive newsletters and can attend workshops and conferences.

The minimum formal educational requirement for curators is a bachelor's degree in one of the biological sciences, such as zoology, ecology, biology, mammalogy, and ornithology. Coursework should include biology, invertebrate zoology, vertebrate physiology, comparative anatomy, organic chemistry, physics, microbiology, and virology. Electives are just as important, particularly writing, public speaking, computer science, and education. Even studying a second language can be helpful.

Typically, an advanced degree is required for curators employed at larger institutions; many curators are required to have a doctoral degree. But advanced academic training alone is insufficient; it takes years of on-the-job experience to master the practical aspects of exotic animal husbandry. Also required are management skills, supervisory experience, writing ability, research experience, and sometimes the flexibility to travel.

Many college professors use zoos and aquariums for research studies. College students can collaborate with in-house research and conservation staff, gaining valuable experience and establishing important contacts.

A few institutions offer curatorial internships designed to provide practical experience. Several major zoos offer formal keeper training courses as well as on-the-job training programs to students who are studying areas related to animal science and care. Such programs could lead to positions as assistant curators. Contact the AZA for further information about which schools and animal facilities are involved in internship programs.

Curators who work for zoos and aquariums must have a fondness and compassion for animals. But as managers of people, strong interpersonal skills are extremely important for curators, including conflict management and negotiating. Curators spend a lot of time making deals with people inside and outside of their institutions. They must have recognized leadership ability, good coaching skills, and the ability to create and maintain a team atmosphere and build consensus.

"I want the staff to be happy in their jobs, to feel a sense of fulfillment and accomplishment. That way the animals will be well cared for," said Anita Cramm, curator of birds at the Phoenix Zoo in Arizona. "I spend a lot of time talking to the keepers, brainstorming with them, responding to their problems. It's a very important part of all our programs."

Curators also need excellent oral and written communication skills. They must be effective and articulate public speakers. They need to be good at problem solving.

Curators should have an in-depth knowledge of every species and exhibit in their collection and how they interact. Modern zoo and aquarium buildings contain technologically advanced, complex equipment, such as environmental controls, and often house mixed species exhibits. Not only must curators know about zoology and animal husbandry, but they must understand the infrastructure as well.

Opportunities for Experience and Exploration

Young people who are interested in pursuing a career as a zoo or aquarium curator should take courses related to animals, such as biology and zoology. Students interested in working in aquariums should set up coral reefs or tanks where they can raise fish at home. Performing volunteer work at animal shelters is an excellent way to gain much-needed practical experience in caring for various types of animals. High school students could also attempt to get part-time jobs working with animals.

The AZA offers practical advice for students who are interested in exploring animal facility jobs such as that of a curator: visit zoos and learn how they operate; try to decide on a specific interest; attend events and meetings planned by zoos and aquariums in your area; and continue to read books on animals and nature.

Methods of Entering

The position of zoo and aquarium curator is seldom an entry level job. Although there are exceptions, most curators start their careers as zookeepers or *aquarists* and move up through the animal management ranks.

"Learn as much as you can, and don't try to move up too quickly," advises Cramm. "Let the hands-on care teach you before you get into decision-making. Once you're there, you can never go back."

Although the competition for zoo and aquarium jobs is intense, there are several ways to pursue such positions. Getting an education in animal science is a good way to make contacts that may be valuable in a job search. Professors and school administrators often can provide advice and counseling on finding jobs as a curator. The best sources for finding out about career opportunities at zoos and aquariums are trade journals (AZA's *Communiqué* or AAZK's *Animal Keepers' Forum*), the Web sites of specific institutions, and special focus periodicals. Most zoos and aquariums have internal job postings. A few zoos and aquariums have job lines. People in the profession often learn about openings by word of mouth.

Working on a part-time or volunteer basis at an animal facility could provide an excellent opportunity to improve eligibility for higher-level jobs in later years. Although many curators have worked in other positions in other fields before obtaining their jobs at animal facilities, others began their careers in lower-level jobs at such places and worked their way up to where they wanted to be.

Moving up from a supervisory keeper position to a curatorial job usually involves moving out to another institution, often in another city and state.

Advancement

Curatorial positions are often the top rung of the career ladder for many zoo and aquarium professionals. Curators do not necessarily wish to become zoo or aquarium directors, although the next step for specialized curators is to advance to the position of general curator. Those who are willing to forego direct involvement with animal management altogether and complete the transition to the business of running a zoo or aquarium will set zoo or aquarium director as their ultimate goal. Curators who work for a small facility may aspire to a curatorial position at a larger zoo or aquarium, with greater responsibilities and a commensurate increase in pay.

Advancing to executive positions requires a combination of experience and education. General curators and zoo directors often have graduate degrees in zoology or in business or finance. Continuing professional education, such as AZA's courses in applied zoo and aquarium biology, conservation education, institutional record keeping, population management, and professional management, can be helpful. Attending workshops and conferences sponsored by professional groups or related organizations and making presentations is another means of networking with colleagues from other institutions and professions and becoming better known within the zoo world.

Employment Outlook

There are fewer than two hundred professionally operated zoos, aquariums, wildlife parks, and oceanariums in North America. Considering the number of people interested in animal careers, this is not a large number. Therefore, it is expected that competition for jobs as curators (as well as for most zoo and aquarium jobs) will continue to be very strong.

The employment outlook for zoo curators is not favorable. Because of the slow growth in new zoos and in their capacity to care for animals, job openings are not expected to grow rapidly. The prospects for aquarium curators is somewhat better due to planned construction of several new aquariums.

However, competition and low turnover rates will continue to squelch opportunities in these occupations. According to Pate, one area with greater growth potential than conventional zoos and aquariums is privately funded conservation centers.

Earnings

Salaries of zoo and aquarium curators are widely varied, depending on the size and location of the institution, whether it is privately or publicly owned, the size of its endowments and budget, and on the curators' responsibilities, educational background, and experience. Generally zoos and aquariums in metropolitan areas pay higher salaries.

Generalizations can be made, however. Yearly salaries for curators range from as low as $20,000 to as high as $79,000 for general curators in major metropolitan areas; average earnings are about $40,000.

Most zoos and aquariums provide benefits packages including medical insurance, paid vacation and sick leave, and generous retirement benefits. As salaried employees, curators are not eligible for overtime pay, but they may get compensatory time for extra hours worked. Larger institutions may also offer coverage for prescription drugs, dental and vision insurance, mental health plans, and retirement savings plans. Private corporate zoos may offer better benefits, including profit sharing.

Conditions of Work

The work atmosphere for curators of animal facilities will always center on the zoo or aquarium in which they work. Curators spend most of their time indoors at their desks, reading email and on the phone, writing reports, meeting deadlines for budgets, planning exhibits, and so forth. Particularly at large institutions, the majority of their time is spent on administrative duties rather than hands-on interaction with animals. Like other zoo and aquarium employees, curators often work long hours tending to the varied duties to which they are assigned.

Went the unexpected happens, curators still get their share of animal emergencies. In difficult situations, they may find themselves working late into the night with keepers and veterinarians to help care for sick animals or those that are giving birth.

Celeste Lombardi, Living Collection Director at the Columbus Zoo in Ohio, told of an animal shipment that went awry. Two eight-month-old lions had been imported from South Africa through New York City on their way to Columbus when their connecting flight was delayed and then cancelled due to inclement weather. Concerned that the animals had already been crated with only water for sixteen hours, Lombardi made numerous calls to arrange the services of an animal broker and to charter a plane, and, along with the assistant zoo director, stayed up until 3:00 AM when the lions finally arrived at their destination.

Curators are sometimes required to travel to conferences and community events. They might also travel to other zoos throughout the country or lead trips for zoo members to wilderness areas in the United States and abroad.

Despite the tedium and the long hours, zoo and aquarium curators derive great personal satisfaction from their work. "Ours is a family-oriented business," said Lombardi. "People come to zoos to learn—whether they're kids or they're ninety years old. I feel that we're doing something good for the earth."

Sources of Additional Information

American Zoo and Aquarium Association
7970-D Old Georgetown Road
Bethesda, MD 20814-2493
WWW: http://www.aza.org/

American Association of Zoo Keepers, Inc.
Topeka Zoological Park
635 Southwest Gage Boulevard
Topeka, KS 66606-2066
Tel: 785-273-1980
WWW: http://aazk.ind.net/

For information regarding schools with animal management curricula, contact:

Friends University of Wichita
2100 W. University
Wichita, KS 67213
Tel: 316-295-5890/1-800-794-6945, x5890
WWW: http://www.friends.edu/natsci/zoo.htm

Santa Fe Community College
Zoo Studies Programs (BS and MS programs)
3000 Northwest 83rd Street
Gainesville, FL 32606
Tel: 352-395-5604
WWW: http://www.aazk.ind.net/aazk/SantaFe.html

Zoo and Aquarium Directors

School Subjects

Biology
Business
English (writing/literature)
Speech

Personal Interests

Animals
Business
Business management
The Environment
Wildlife

Work Environment

Primarily indoors
Primarily one location

Minimum Education Level

Bachelor's degree

Salary Range

$28,000 to $100,000+

Certification or Licensing

None

Outlook

Little change or more slowly than the average

DOT

102

GOE

11.02.01

NOC

0212

Definition

Zoo and aquarium directors, or *chief executive officers*, are administrators who coordinate the business affairs of these centers. Like all executives, they have diverse responsibilities. Directors execute the institution's policies, usually under the direction of a governing authority. They are responsible for the institution's operation and plans for future development and for such tasks as fund-raising and public relations. They also serve as representatives of, and advocates for, their institution and their entire industry.

History

Zoos and aquariums have undergone a revolution in recent times. Modern zoos are very different from the menageries of yesteryear, where the emphasis was on displaying and caring for as many species as possible for the amusement of visitors, with little concern for the context in which the animals were presented. Today's zoos and aquariums are built around habitat-based, multi-species exhibits designed to immerse the visitor in an experience simulating a visit to the wild places from which the animals come. The keeping and breeding of captive animals is no longer an end in itself, but a means of educating and communicating a strong conservation imperative to the public. The public has embraced this change, with visitor numbers rising steadily each year.

Along with this expanded public role has come a professionalization of the industry, marked by advances in animal husbandry, veterinary care, nutrition, and exhibit technology that have greatly improved the conditions under which animals are held. These advances have been costly, and the rise in operating expenses reflects these increased costs. Zoos and aquariums today are big business.

Traditionally, most zoo and aquarium directors came straight from the animal management staff, working their way up through the ranks from *zookeeper* or *aquarist* to *curator* to director. Some zoo and aquarium curators still become directors. However, the director's job has changed radically in the past fifteen years, reflecting the overall maturity of the zoo and aquarium business. Directors no longer have direct responsibility for working with animals or managing the people who care for them. The director's role has broadened from animal management to overall management. Their focus has shifted from internal issues to external ones. Rather than concentrate on day-to-day details of running the facility, the modern director must concentrate on the big picture.

Nature of the Work

Directors of zoos and aquariums are considered administrative personnel. Their job is like that of the president of a company or the principal of a school; that is, they are responsible mainly for the important business affairs of the institution.

Working under the supervision of a governing board, directors are charged with pulling together all the institution's operations, development of long-range planning, implementation of new programs, and maintenance of the animal collection and facilities. Much of the director's time is spent interfacing with the volunteer governing board to whom he or she reports and with departmental staff, who handle the institution's daily operations.

Directors are responsible for planning overall budgets, which includes consideration of fund-raising programs; government grants; and private financial support from corporations, foundations, and individuals. They work with the board of directors to design major policies and procedures, and they meet with the curators to discuss animal acquisitions, public education, research projects, and developmental activities. In larger zoos and aquariums, directors may give speeches, appear at fund-raising events, and represent their organizations on television or radio.

"Zoos and aquariums are mission-driven, which opens the door to more diverse responsibilities," said Kathryn Roberts, Ph.D., Executive Director of the Minnesota Zoo in Apple Valley, Minnesota. "The CEO of a major corporation is responsible only to the stockholders. We have a huge group of constituents, each with different needs."

A major part of the director's job is seeing that his or her institution has adequate financial resources. Where zoos and aquariums were once funded largely by local and state governments, the amount of tax money available for this purpose is dwindling. Generally, zoos and aquariums need to generate enough revenue to pay for about two-thirds of their operating expenses from sources such as donations, membership, retail sales, and visitor services.

As zoos and aquariums endeavor to improve facilities for animals and visitors alike and to present the conservation message to the public in a more effective manner, renovation of existing structures and construction of new exhibits is on ongoing process. Directors spend much of their time working with architects, engineers, contractors, and artisans on these projects.

Directors are responsible for informing the public about what is going on at the zoo or aquarium. This involves interviews with the media, answering questions from individuals, and even resolving complaints. The director is the face—and the voice—that represents his or her institution to the public. In addition to being interviewed by journalists and other writers, directors do writing of their own: for in-house newsletters and annual reports or for general circulation magazines and newspapers.

Although not directly involved in animal management within his or her own institution, the director may play a significant role in conservation at a regional, national, or international level. Directors work on committees for various conservation organizations, such as the more than eighty American Zoo and Aquarium Association (AZA) Species Survival Plans (SSP) that target individual species for intense conservation efforts by zoos and aquariums. They may be involved at a higher level of the AZA, working on such things as accreditation of other institutions, developing professional ethics, or long-range planning. Directors work with other conservation groups as well and may serve in leadership positions for them too.

As zoos and aquariums expand their conservation role from only the management of captive animals to supporting the preservation of the habitats those animals came from, directors are working with universities and field biologists to support research.

Within their own zoo or aquarium, directors may work with other volunteer boards whose purpose is to raise money. They attend numerous social gatherings, including fund-raising events for their institution, and community events. Directors are constantly networking, always on the lookout for people who want to support their institutions in one way or another.

Because of their exposure and the public's fascination with animals, zoo and aquariums directors often become local or national celebrities.

Other directorial personnel include *assistant directors* and *deputy directors*. Like curators, these workers are responsible for a specific duty or department, such as operations, education, or animal management. They also manage certain employees, supervise animal care workers, and take care of various administrative duties to help the director.

Requirements

Students who aspire to upper level management in zoos and aquariums should get a multi-disciplinary education. As the director's job has evolved beyond a narrow animal management focus, so too has the career path to that job. While a knowledge of zoology is important for anyone interested in working at a zoo or aquarium, students should remember that experts in other areas of management can move into the director's chair.

"Zoos are not just about animal keeping," said Brian Rutledge, President/CEO of Zoo New England in Boston, Massachusetts. "Discover what skills are best for you, accentuate them, and aim them at a zoo and conservation. Everyone has a skill they can bring to the team."

Volunteering at a zoo or aquarium provides the opportunity to learn how the institution works and to target a particular area of interest. Other extracurricular activities for students interested in becoming zoo and aquarium directors should focus on developing leadership and communications skills: student body associations, service clubs, debate teams, and school newspapers.

Because competition for jobs is fierce, students need to get good grades.

A director's education and experience must be rather broad, with a solid foundation in animal management skills. Therefore, a good balance between science and business is the key to finding a position in this field. Directors need courses in zoology or biology as well as business courses, such as economics, accounting, and general business courses, and humanities, like sociology.

Today most directors have a master's degree; many at larger institutions have doctorate degrees. Directors continue their education throughout their careers by taking classes, as well as reading and learning on their own.

Zoo and aquarium directors are leaders and communicators. Inspiring others and promoting their institution are among their most important tasks. Their most important traits include leadership ability, personal charisma, people skills, and public speaking ability.

"The director must have the ability to craft a vision, to own it, to guard it, and to promote it," said Terry L. Maple, Ph.D., President and Chief Executive Officer of Zoo Atlanta in Georgia. "A director has to focus on the vision, believe in it, and get others to do so."

Directors need to be politically saavy. They interact with many different groups, each with their own agenda: the institution's governing board; its staff (animal management, operations, education, conservation, marketing, development, human resources, and so forth); local, state, and federal politicians; foundations; corporate and individual donors; members; schools; visitors; even animal rights organizations. Directors must be able to build bridges between these various groups and put together a consensus. They need to be flexible and open-minded without losing sight of their role as advocate for their institution.

Directors must have outstanding time management skills, and they must be willing and able to delegate. The best directors need to know their own weaknesses and hire people who can compensate in those areas, according to Jane Ballentine, Director of Public Affairs for the American Zoo and Aquarium Association.

A fondness and compassion for animals is not all that is needed to become a successful zoo or aquarium director. "Too many people get into the business because they like animals," said Tony Vecchio, Director of the Metro Washington Park Zoo in Portland, Oregon. "The zoo business is not just animals; it's all about people. Education may not be as exciting as breeding endangered species or supporting in situ research, but it is our best contribution to conservation."

Directors must be articulate and sociable. They must be able to communicate effectively with people from all walks of life. Much of their time is spent cultivating prospective donors. They must be comfortable with many different types of people, including those with wealth and power.

The director's job is a round-the-clock commitment. This is not a career for someone unwilling to work very hard.

Opportunities for Experience and Exploration

Young people who are interested in pursuing a career as a zoo or aquarium director should take courses related to animals, such as biology and zoology. Performing volunteer work at animal shelters is an excellent way to gain practical experience in caring for various types of animals. High school students could also attempt to get part-time jobs at zoos, kennels, pet stores, stables, veterinary facilities, or animal adoption facilities.

Professional organizations, such as the AZA and the American Association of Zoo Keepers, Inc. (AAZK), have special membership rates for nonprofessionals. Associate members receive newsletters and can attend workshops and conferences. Students interested in careers at zoos and aquariums should join these organizations to learn more about the field.

AZA offers practical advice for students who are considering animal facility jobs such as that of the director. Suggestions for exploration include visiting zoos and aquariums and learning how they operate; trying to decide on a specific interest; attending events and meetings planned by zoos and aquariums in your area; and continuing to read books and journals on animals and nature.

Students interested in the business side of zoo and aquarium operations should concentrate on developing skills related to a particular area of expertise, such as public relations, marketing, human resources, and so forth.

Methods of Entering

The position of zoo and aquarium director is not an entry level job. Achieving a position at this level requires focus, determination, ambition, and long-range career planning. Aspiring directors should set their goals high and constantly strive to do their best. This is not a career for someone unwilling to take the steps required to stand out above the crowd.

Although the competition for zoo and aquarium jobs is stiff, there are several ways to pursue such positions. Some animal facilities offer internships to students who are studying areas related to animal science and care; contact the AZA for further information about which schools and animal facilities are involved in internship programs. Other zoo and aquarium jobs can also start a student on the way to becoming a director.

The best sources for finding out about career opportunities at zoos and aquariums are trade journals (such as AZA's *Communiqué* or AAZK's *Animal Keepers' Forum*), the Web sites of specific institutions, and special focus periodicals. Most zoos and aquariums have internal job postings. Institutions seeking candidates for high level positions, such as the director's, sometimes use executive search firms. People in the profession often learn about openings by word of mouth.

Whatever a student's particular interest is, he or she must pursue that specialty within the zoo and aquarium setting. Among today's zoo and aquarium directors are people who began their careers in education, marketing, business, research, and academia, as well as animal management.

Advancement

The position of zoo and aquarium director is the top rung of the career ladder that many animal science students pursue. Because directors are considered high-level employees at animal facilities, if they wish to advance, they may consider moving from zoos to aquariums (or vice versa) or going on to a different field altogether. Or, if they work for a small facility, they may try to secure a position at a larger zoo or aquarium. Many young directors have established their reputations by rebuilding an institution with outmoded facilities or severe financial problems.

Although some directors may move about, the majority remain at the same institution, reflecting the strong identification of the director with the institution that he or she leads.

Employment Outlook

There are fewer than two hundred professionally operated zoos, aquariums, wildlife parks, and oceanariums in North America. Each of them employs only one director. Therefore, competition for jobs as directors (as well as for zoo and aquarium jobs in general) is expected to remain very strong.

Generally, the employment outlook for directors is not favorable. Because of the slow growth in the number of new zoos, job openings are not expected to grow. The continuing competition and low turnover rates will increasingly decrease the number of opportunities. The outlook for aquariums is somewhat brighter due to the planned construction of several new facilities.

Earnings

Salaries of zoo and aquarium directors vary widely, depending on the size and location of the institution, whether it is publicly or privately owned, the size of its endowments and budget, and on the director's responsibilities, educational background, and experience. Generally zoos and aquariums in metropolitan areas pay higher salaries.

Directors tend to be the highest paid employees at zoos and aquariums; the range of their salary is also broad, from $28,000 to more than $100,000 per year, with some directors at major institutions earning considerably more than that. Given the scope of their responsibilities, salaries are not very high.

Most zoos and aquariums provide benefits packages including medical insurance, paid vacation and sick leave, and generous retirement benefits. Larger institutions may also offer coverage for prescription drugs, dental and vision insurance, mental health plans, and 401(k) plans. Private corporate zoos may offer better benefits, including profit sharing.

Some directors supplement their regular salaries with income from books and paid public speaking engagements.

Conditions of Work

The zoo and aquarium director's job is very demanding and time consuming. The challenges of running a large, multifaceted institution never go away. All directors take work home with them, such as reading and correspondence; most have computers and offices in their homes.

Nonetheless, the daily responsibilities of directors of zoos and aquariums generally center on the facility in which they work. Directors tend to spend a great deal of time in their offices conducting business affairs. They attend a lot of meetings. "The director's job is not for those who need a daily fix with animals," said Dr. Maple.

Directors are sometimes required to travel to conferences and community events. They might also travel to other institutions throughout the country or abroad to attend meetings of professional organizations and conservation groups or to discuss animal transfers and other matters. Often, directors lead groups on trips around the United States or to developing countries.

Sources of Additional Information

American Zoo and Aquarium Association
7970-D Old Georgetown Road
Bethesda, MD 20814-2493
WWW: http://www.aza.org/

American Association of Zoo Keepers, Inc.
Topeka Zoological Park
635 Southwest Gage Boulevard
Topeka, KS 66606-2066
Tel: 785-273-1980
WWW: http://aazk.ind.net/

Zookeepers

School Subjects
Biology
Computer science
English (writing/literature)
Speech

Personal Interests
Animals
The Environment
Wildlife

Work Environment
Indoors and outdoors
Primarily one location

Minimum Education Level
Bachelor's degree

Salary Range
$14,000 to $27,000 to $40,000+

Certification or Licensing
None

Outlook
About as fast as the average

DOT
412

GOE
03.03.02

NOC
6483

Definition

Zookeepers provide the day-to-day care for animals in zoological parks. They prepare the diets, clean and maintain the exhibits and holding areas, and monitor the behavior of animals that range from the exotic and endangered to the more common and domesticated. *Aquarists* provide day-to-day care for fishes or marine mammals and birds in aquariums. They prepare diets; clean and maintain tanks, equipment, and plants; and monitor the behavior of the animals in their care. Keepers and aquarists interact with visitors and conduct formal and informal educational presentations, sometimes assist in research studies and, depending upon the species, may also train animals.

History

Humans have put wild animals on display since ancient times. About 1500 BC, Queen Hatshepsut of Egypt established the earliest known zoo. Five hundred years later, the Chinese emperor Wen Wang founded a zoo that covered about fifteen hundred acres. Rulers seeking to display their wealth and power established small zoos in northern Africa, India, and China.

The ancient Greeks established public zoos, while the Romans had many private zoos. During the Middle Ages, from about AD 400 to 1500, zoos became rare in Europe.

By the end of the 1400s, European explorers returned from the New World with strange animals, and interest in zoos renewed. During the next 250 years, a number of zoos were established. Some merely consisted of small collections of bears or tigers kept in dismal cages or pits. They were gradually replaced by larger collections of animals that received better care.

In 1752, what is now the oldest zoo, the Schönbrunn, opened in Vienna, Austria. Other European zoos followed. In the United States, the Central Park Zoo in New York City opened in 1864, followed by the Buffalo Zoo in New York in 1870, and Chicago's Lincoln Park Zoo in 1874.

Workers were needed to care for the animals in even the earliest zoos. However, this care probably consisted only of giving the animals food and water and cleaning their cages. Little was known about the needs of a particular species, for if an animal died, it could be replaced by another animal from the wild. Few zoos owned more than one or two animals of a rare species, so the keepers did not need to be involved in observations or research on an animal's lifestyle, health, or nutrition.

The modern zoo and aquarium is a far cry from even the menageries of earlier eras. Today's zoos and aquariums are still in the entertainment field, but they have assumed three additional roles: conservation, education, and research. Each of these roles has become vital due to the increasing pressures on the world's wildlife.

Nature of the Work

The zookeeper or aquarist is responsible for providing the basic care required to maintain the health of the animals in his or her charge. Daily tasks include preparing food by chopping or grinding meat, fish, vegetables, or fruit; mixing prepared commercial feeds; and unbaling forage grasses. Administering vitamins or medications may be necessary as well. In addition, zookeepers fill water containers in the cages. They clean animal quarters by hosing, scrubbing, raking, and disinfecting.

Zookeepers must safely shift animals from one location to another. They maintain exhibits (for example, by planting grass or putting in new bars) and modify them to enhance the visitors' experience. They also provide enrichment devices for the animals, such as ropes for monkeys to swing on or scratching areas for big cats. They regulate environmental factors by monitoring temperature and humidity or water quality controls and maintain an inventory of supplies and equipment. They may bathe and groom animals.

Zookeepers and aquarists must become experts on the species—and the individuals—in their care. They must observe and understand all types of animal behaviors, including courtship, mating, feeding, aggression, sociality, sleeping, moving, and even urination and defecation. Keepers and aquarists must be able to detect even small changes in an animal's appearance or behavior. They must maintain careful records of these observations in a logbook and file daily written or computerized reports. Often, they make recommendations regarding diet or modification of habitats and implement those changes. In addition, they assist the veterinarian in providing treatment to sick animals and may be called upon to feed and help raise infants. Keepers and aquarists may capture or transport animals. When an animal is transferred to another institution, a keeper may accompany it to aid in its adjustment to its new home.

The professional zookeeper works closely with zoo staff on research, conservation, and animal reproduction. Many keepers conduct research projects, presenting their findings in papers or professional journals or at workshops or conferences. Some keepers participate in regional or national conservation plans or conduct field research in the United States and abroad.

Keepers may assist an *animal trainer* or instructor in presenting animal shows or lectures to the public. Depending on the species, keepers may train animals to shift or to move in a certain way to facilitate routine husbandry or veterinary care. Elephant keepers, for example, train their charges to respond to commands to lift their feet so that they may provide proper foot care including foot pad and toenail trims.

Zookeepers must be able to interact with zoo visitors and answer questions in a friendly, professional manner. Keepers may participate in formal presentations for the general public or for special groups. This involves being knowledgeable about the animals in one's care, the animals' natural habitat and habits, and the role zoos play in wildlife conservation.

Keepers must carefully monitor activity around the animals to discourage visitors from teasing or harming them. They must be able to remove harmful objects that are sometimes thrown into an exhibit and tactfully explain the "no feeding" policy to zoo visitors.

Taking care of animals is hard work. About 85 percent of the job involves custodial and maintenance tasks, which can be physically demanding and dirty. These tasks must be done both indoors and outdoors, in all types of weather. In addition, there is the risk of an animal-inflicted injury or disease. Although direct contact with animals is limited and strictly managed, the possibility for injury exists when a person is working with large, powerful animals or even small animals that possess sharp teeth and claws.

Because animals require care every day, keepers and aquarists must work weekends and holidays. They may also be called upon to work special events outside their normal working hours.

In large zoological parks, keepers often work with a limited collection of animals. They may be assigned to work specifically with just one taxon, such as primates, large cats, or birds, or with different types of animals from a specific ecogeographic area, such as the Tropical Rainforest or the Apes of Africa. In smaller zoos, keepers may have more variety and care for a wider range of species.

Requirements

Students planning a career in zookeeping should take as many science classes in high school as possible. A broad-based science education including courses in biology, ecology, chemistry, physics, and botany, coupled with mathematics and computer science is best. Courses in English and speech develop vocabulary and hone public speaking skills.

Activities such as reading about animals or surfing the Internet; taking classes at local zoos and aquariums; or joining clubs, such as 4-H, Audubon, or local herpetological societies, can help students learn about animals. Students interested in careers as aquarists should raise fish and even get some diving experience. Volunteering at zoos or aquariums—or animal shelters, boarding kennels, wildlife facilities, stables, or animal hospitals—demonstrates a serious commitment to animals and provides first-hand experience with them.

Professional organizations, such as the American Zoo and Aquarium Association (AZA) and the American Association of Zoo Keepers, Inc. (AAZK), have special membership rates for nonprofessionals. Associate members receive newsletters and can attend workshops and conferences.

Although practical experience may sometimes be substituted for formal education, most entry level positions require a four-year college degree. Animal management has become a highly technical and specialized field. Zookeepers and aquarists do much more than care for animals' bodily comforts: today's zookeepers are *zoologists*. They must be able to perform detailed behavioral observations, recordkeeping, nutrition studies, and health care. Their increased responsibilities make their role an essential one in maintaining a healthy animal collection.

Degrees in animal science, zoology, marine biology, conservation biology, wildlife management, or animal behavior are preferred. Electives are just as important, particularly writing, public speaking, computer science, education—even additional languages. Applicants with interdisciplinary training sometimes have an advantage. A few colleges and junior colleges offer a specialized curriculum for zookeepers. Those seeking advancement to curatorial, research, or conservation positions may need a master's degree. Animal care experience such as *zoo volunteer, farm or ranch worker*, or *veterinary hospital worker* is a must.

Many college professors use zoos and aquariums for research studies. College students can collaborate with in-house research and conservation staff on subjects ranging from observations of typical behaviors in polar bears to precise measurement of preferred food items of birds in a mixed-species free flight exhibit.

Smaller zoos may hire *keeper trainees*, who receive on-the-job training to learn the responsibilities of the zookeeper. Several major zoos offer formal keeper training courses, as well as on-the-job training programs, to students who are studying areas related to animal science and care; contact AZA for further information about which schools and animal facilities are involved in internship programs. Such programs could lead to full time positions.

Many institutions offer unpaid internships for high school and college students interested in investigating a career in animal care. Internships may involve food preparation, hands-on experience with the animal collection, interpretive services for the public, exhibit design and construction, or the collection and analysis of data. The length of the internships varies. The minimum age for most of these programs is eighteen.

Generally, no certification or licensing is required. However, aquarists or zookeepers working with marine mammals may be required to have a SCUBA or CPR certification or pass a swimming test.

Some zoos require written aptitude tests or oral exams. Applicants must pass a physical exam, as keepers must be physically able to do such demanding work as lifting heavy sacks of feed or moving sick or injured animals.

Union membership is more common at publicly operated zoos, but it is on the rise in privately run institutions as well. There is no single zookeepers' union, and a variety of different unions represent the employees at various zoos and aquariums.

Zookeepers and aquarists must first and foremost have a fondness and empathy for animals. "I always had a passion for animals. I liked watching them and working with them," said Ron Ringer, a senior keeper at the

Zoological Society of San Diego, who has worked with elephants and rhinoceroses for eighteen years. "I was always bringing home something I wasn't supposed to."

The work of the zookeeper and aquarist is not glamorous. It takes a special kind of dedication to provide care to captive animals that require attention twenty-four hours a day, 365 days a year.

Keepers and aquarists need excellent interpersonal skills to work together and to interact with visitors and volunteers. Strong oral and written communication skills are also required. They should be detail oriented and enjoy paperwork and record keeping.

They must be able to work well independently and as part of a team. Keepers rely on each other to get their job done safely.

A calm, stable nature, maturity, good judgment, and the ability to adhere to established animal handling and/or safety procedures is essential. Being in a bad mood can interfere with concentration, endangering the keeper and his or her coworkers.

Keepers and aquarists must have keen powers of observation. "The keepers that stand out develop a sixth sense that's hard to describe and difficult to learn," said Lucy Segerson, a zookeeper at the North Carolina Zoological Park in Asheboro. "Often, exotic animals don't show that they're in trouble until it's too late. But with experience with different species and individuals, you learn to see those subtle little changes that indicate an animal is sick."

Due to the physical demands of the job, keepers and aquarists must be physically fit. Psychological fitness is important too. Zookeepers and aquarists have to be able to handle the emotional impact when animals with whom they have built a relationship go to another institution or die. They can't be squeamish about handling body wastes or live food items or dealing with sick animals.

Zookeeper applicants must be persistent. They may face many rejections before they land their first job.

Opportunities for Experience and Exploration

High school students can explore the field of animal care in several ways. They can learn about animals by reading about them and taking classes in biology and zoology. Most zoos and aquariums have Web sites containing information about the institution and its programs and career opportunities, as well as about the industry in general. Hobbies such as birding expand the knowledge of animals.

Many institutions offer classes about animals and conservation or educational programs like Keeper Encounters, where students can learn first hand what a zookeeper's job is like.

Some have part time or summer jobs that can give a good overview of how a zoo operates. Many zoos and aquariums offer volunteer opportunities for teens, such as Explorers or Junior Zookeeper programs, which are similar to programs for adult volunteers, but with closer supervision. Most volunteer programs require a specific time commitment. Opportunities vary between institutions, and run the gamut from cleaning enclosures to preparing food to handling domesticated animals to conducting tours or giving educational presentations.

Prospective zookeepers and aquarists can volunteer or work part time at animal shelters, boarding kennels, wildlife rehabilitation facilities, stables, or animal hospitals. They may get a feel for working with animals by seeking employment on a farm or ranch during the summer. Joining a 4-H club also gives a person hands-on experience with animals. Experience with animals is invaluable when seeking a job and provides opportunities to learn about the realities of work in this field.

Professional organizations have special membership rates for nonprofessionals. Reading their newsletters provides an insider's look at what zoo and aquarium careers are like. Attending local workshops or national conferences offers an opportunity to network and gather information for charting a career path.

Methods of Entering

Despite the low pay and challenging working conditions, competition for jobs at zoos and aquariums is intense. There are many more candidates than available positions. Most zookeepers and aquarists enjoy their work, and turnover is low. The majority of new jobs results from the need to replace workers who leave the field. A limited number of jobs are created when new zoos and aquariums open. Entry level applicants may find it easier to start out in small zoos in smaller communities, where the pay is usually low, and then move on once they have gained some experience. There are many such small town zoos in the Midwest.

The days when zookeepers were hired off the street and trained on the job are a thing of the past. Today, most institutions require a bachelor's degree. But "a classical education alone is not enough," according to Brian

Rutledge, President/CEO of Zoo New England in Boston, Massachusetts. Practical experience working with animals is a must. This experience can involve volunteering at a zoo or wildlife rehabilitation center, caring for animals in a kennel or animal hospital, or working on a farm or ranch.

Part-time work, summer jobs, or volunteering at a zoo or aquarium increases an applicant's chances of getting full time employment. Many zoos fill new positions by promoting current employees. An entry level position, even if it does not involve working directly with animals, is a means of making contacts and learning about an institution's hiring practices.

"Start out working at guest services or driving the safari van," Jane Ballentine, director of public affairs for AZA, advises. "You get your foot in the door, meet the people, and find out if this is a place you would like to work." Zoos and aquariums that are municipally operated accept applications through municipal civil service offices. At other zoos, application is made directly at the zoo office.

Occasionally zoos and aquariums advertise for personnel in the local newspapers. A better source of employment opportunities are trade journals (AZA's *Communiqué* or AAZK's *Animal Keepers' Forum*), the Web sites of specific institutions, or special focus periodicals. A few zoos and aquariums have job lines.

Most zoos and aquariums have internal job postings. People in the profession often learn about openings by word of mouth. Membership in a professional organization can be helpful when conducting a job search.

Advancement

Job advancement in zoos is possible but the career path is more limited than in some other professions requiring a college degree. The possibility for advancement varies according to a zoo's size and operating policies and an employee's qualifications.

Continuing professional education is a must to keep current on progress in husbandry, veterinary care, and technology, and in order to advance. AZA offers formal professional courses in applied zoo and aquarium biology, conservation education, elephant management, institutional record keeping, population management, professional management, and studbook keeping. Attending workshops and conferences sponsored by professional groups or related organizations, such as universities or conservation organizations, is another means of sharing information with colleagues from other institutions and professions.

Most zoos and aquariums have different levels of animal management staff. The most common avenue for job promotion is from keeper to senior keeper to head keeper, then possibly to area supervisor or assistant curator and then curator. On rare occasions, the next step will be to zoo or aquarium director. Moving up from the senior keeper level to middle and upper management usually involves moving out to another institution, often in another city and state.

In addition to participating in daily animal care, the senior keeper manages a particular building on the zoo grounds and is responsible for supervising the keepers working in that facility. An area supervisor or assistant curator works directly with the curators and is responsible for supervising, scheduling, and training the entire keeper force. In major zoological parks, there are head keepers for each curatorial department.

The curator is responsible for managing a specific department or section within the zoo, either defined by taxon, such as mammals, birds, reptiles, etc., or by habitat or ecogeography, such as the Forest Edge or African Savannah. The curator of mammals, for example, is in charge of all mammals in the collection and supervises all staff who work with mammals. Usually, an advanced degree in zoology and research experience is required to become a curator, as well as experience working as a zookeeper and in zoo management.

Many zookeepers and aquarists eschew advancement and prefer to remain in work where they have the most direct interaction with and impact on the animals.

Employment Outlook

Zoos hire more animal keepers than any other classification. But this is still a very small job pool. Of the more than 17,000 professionals working in zoos and aquariums, fewer than 6,000 are keepers and aquarists. Approximately 350 zookeeper jobs become available each year in the United States. There are many more applicants than positions available. Competition for jobs is stiff in the nearly 200 professionally operated zoological parks, aquariums, and wildlife parks in North America.

But the outlook is growing, according to Ballentine, particularly for aquariums. Opportunities arise mainly through attrition, which is lower than in many other professions, or the startup of a new facility. The opening in 1998 of Disney's Animal Kingdom and the Long Beach Aquarium created a ripple effect throughout the entire industry as experienced personnel migrated to Florida and California, respectively, and jobs for new hires and promotions opened up at dozens of institutions. Many more new aquariums are planned or under construction, including in Gatlinburg, Tennessee; Niagara, New York; Denver and Fort Collins, Colorado; and Toronto, Ontario. Jobs for zookeepers will grow more slowly as institutions expand their exhibits and programs, particularly those related to conservation and education.

Aspiring zookeepers and aquarists are not the only ones who will benefit. "Ten years ago, there were no geneticists in zoos and there were very few people working in conservation departments, public relations, or development," said Anita Cramm, curator of birds at the Phoenix Zoo in Arizona. "Fifteen years ago, there were no education departments. As zoos continue to grow, new career opportunities will emerge."

As the preservation of animal species becomes more complicated, there will be a continuing need for zoo staff to work to preserve endangered wildlife and educate the public about conservation. The demand will increase for well-educated personnel who will be responsible for much more than simply feeding the animals and cleaning their enclosures. Zookeepers will need more knowledge as zoos expand and become more specialized. The amount of knowledge and effort necessary to maintain and reproduce a healthy animal collection will keep zookeepers and aquarists in the front line of animal care.

Pursuing a job in this area is well worth the effort for those who are dedicated to providing care for rapidly diminishing animal species and educating the public about the fate of endangered animals and the need to preserve their natural habitats.

Earnings

Most people who choose a career as a zookeeper or aquarist do not do so for the money, but because they feel compassion for and enjoy being around animals.

Salaries vary widely among zoological parks and depend upon the size and location of the institution, whether it is publicly or privately owned, the size of its endowments and budget, and whether the zookeepers belong to a union. Generally, the highest salaries tend to be in metropolitan areas and are relative to the applicant's education and responsibilities. The zookeeper's salary can range from slightly above minimum wage to more than $40,000 a year, depending on the keeper's background, grade, and tenure and the zoo's location. Certain areas of the country pay higher wages, reflecting the higher cost of living there. City-run institutions, where keepers are lumped into a job category with lesser skilled workers, pay less. On average, aquarists earn slightly more than zookeepers.

Most zoos and aquariums provide benefits packages including medical insurance, paid vacation and sick leave and generous retirement benefits. Keepers at larger institutions may also have coverage for prescription drugs, dental and vision insurance, mental health plans, and 401(k) plans. Those who work on holidays may receive overtime pay or comp time. A few institutions offer awards, research grants, and unpaid sabbaticals. Private corporate zoos may offer better benefits, including profit sharing.

Conditions of Work

Cleaning, feeding, and providing general care to the animals are a necessity seven days a week, sometimes outdoors and in adverse weather conditions. The zookeeper must be prepared for a varied schedule that may include working weekends and holidays. Sick animals may need round-the-clock care. A large portion of the job involves routine chores for animals that will not express appreciation for the keeper's efforts.

Some of the work may be physically demanding and involve lifting heavy supplies such as bales of hay. The cleaning of an animal's enclosure may be unpleasant and smelly. Between the sounds of the animals and the sounds of the zoo visitors, the work setting may be quite noisy.

The zookeeper may be exposed to bites, kicks, zoonotic diseases, and possible fatal injury from the animals he or she attends. He or she must practice constant caution because working with animals presents the potential for danger. Even though an animal may have been held in captivity for years or even since birth, it can be frightened, become stressed because of illness, or otherwise revert to its wild behavior. The keeper must know the physical and mental abilities of an animal, whether it be the strength of an ape, the reaching ability of a large cat, or the intelligence of an elephant. In addition, they must develop a healthy relationship with the animals in their care by respecting them as individuals and always being careful to observe safety procedures.

Being a zookeeper is an active, demanding job. The tasks involved require agility and endurance, whether they consist of cleaning quarters, preparing food, or handling animals.

Many keepers would agree that the disadvantages of the job are outweighed by the advantages. A chief advantage is the personal gratification of successfully maintaining wild animals, especially rare or endangered species.

A healthy, well-adjusted animal collection provides a keeper with a deep sense of satisfaction.

Sources of Additional Information

American Association of Zoo Keepers, Inc.
Topeka Zoological Park
635 Southwest Gage Boulevard
Topeka, KS 66606-2066
Tel: 785 273-1980
WWW: http://aazk.ind.net/

American Zoo and Aquarium Association
7970-D Old Georgetown Road
Bethesda, MD 20814-2493
WWW: http://www.aza.org/

ZooNet—All About Zoos
WWW: http://www.mindspring.com/~zoonet/

ZooWeb
WWW: http://www.zooweb.net/

Zoologists

Biology Chemistry Computer Science English (writing/literature)	School Subjects
Animals Reading/Books Science Writing	Personal Interests
Indoors and outdoors Primarily one location	Work Environment
Bachelor's degree	Minimum Education Level
$22,000 to $36,300 to $80,000+	Salary Range
None	Certification or Licensing
Faster than the average	Outlook

Definition

Zoologists are biologists who study animals. They often select a particular type of animal to study, and they may study an entire animal, one part or aspect of an animal, or a whole animal society. There are many areas of specialization from which a zoologist can choose, such as origins, genetics, characteristics, classifications, behaviors, life processes, and distribution of animals.

History

Human beings have always studied animals. Knowledge of animal behavior was a necessity to prehistoric humans, whose survival depended on their success in hunting. Those early people who hunted to live learned to respect and even revere their prey. The earliest known paintings, located in the Lascaux Caves in France, depict animals, which demonstrates the importance of animals to early humans. Most experts believe that the artists who painted those images viewed the animals they hunted not just as a food source, but also as an important element of spiritual or religious life.

The first important developments in zoology occurred in Greece, where Alcmaeon, a philosopher and physician, studied animals and performed the first known dissections of humans in the sixth century BC. Aristotle, however, is generally considered to be the first real zoologist. Aristotle (384-322 BC), who studied with the great philosopher Plato and tutored the world-conquering Alexander the Great, had the lofty goal of setting down in writing everything that was known in his time. In an attempt to extend that knowledge, he observed and dissected sea creatures. He also devised a system of classifying animals that included five hundred species—a system that influenced scientists for many centuries after his death. Some scholars believe that Alexander sent various exotic animals to his old tutor from the lands he conquered, giving Aristotle unparalleled access to the animals of the ancient world.

With the exception of important work in physiology done by the Roman physician Galen (AD 129-c.199), the study of zoology progressed little after Aristotle until the middle of the sixteenth century. Between 1555 and 1700, much significant work was done in the classification of species and in physiology, especially regarding the circulation of blood, which affected studies of both animals and humans. The invention of the microscope in approximately 1590 led to the discovery and study of cells. In the eighteenth century, Swedish botanist Carl Linnaeus (1707-1778) developed the system of classification of plants and animals that is still used.

Zoology continued to develop at a rapid rate, and in 1859 Charles Darwin (1809-1882) published his *Origin of Species*, which promoted the theory of natural selection; revolutionized the way scientists viewed all living creatures; and gave rise to the field of ethology, the study of animal behavior. Since that time, innumerable advances have been made by zoologists throughout the world.

In the twentieth century, the rapid development of technology has changed zoology and all sciences by giving scientists the tools to explore areas that had previously been closed to them. Computers, submersibles, spacecraft, and tremendously powerful microscopes are only a few of the means that modern zoologists have used to bring new knowledge to light. In spite of these advances, however, mysteries remain, questions go unanswered, and species wait to be discovered.

Nature of the Work

Although zoology is a single specialty within the field of biology, it is a vast specialty that includes many major subspecialties. Some zoologists study a single animal or a category of animals, whereas others may specialize in a particular part of an animal's anatomy or study a process that takes place in many kinds of animals. A zoologist might study single-cell organisms, a particular variety of fish, or the behavior of groups of animals such as elephants or bees.

Many zoologists are classified according to the animals they study. For example, *entomologists* are experts on insects, *icthyologists* study fish, *herpetologists* specialize in the study of reptiles and amphibians, *mammalogists* focus on mammals, and *ornithologists* study birds. *Embryologists*, however, are classified according to the process that they study. They examine the ways in which animal embryos form and develop, from conception to birth.

Within each primary area of specialization there is a wide range of subspecialties. An ichthyologist, for example, might focus on the physiology, or physical structure and functioning, of a particular fish; on a biochemical phenomenon such as bioluminescence in deep-sea species; on the discovery and classification of fish; on variations within a single species in different parts of the world; or on the ways in which one type of fish interacts with other species in a specific environment. Others may specialize in the effects of pollution on fish or in finding ways to grow fish effectively in controlled environments in order to increase the supply of healthy food available for human consumption.

Some zoologists are primarily teachers, while others spend most of their time performing original research. Teaching jobs in universities and other facilities are probably the most secure positions available, but zoologists who wish to do extensive research may find such positions restrictive. Even zoologists whose primary function is research, however, often need to do some teaching in the course of their work, and almost everyone in the field has to deal with the public at one time or another. As Dr. R. Grant Gilmore, a fish ecologist who is a senior scientist and former director of marine science at the Harbor Branch Oceanographic Institute, says, "In marine science, it's a public day, too. You do get reporters calling about odd things all the time. That happens. People don't realize that, but you end up going before the public eye whether you want to or not."

Students often believe that zoological scientists spend most of their time in the field, observing animals and collecting specimens. In fact, most researchers spend no more than two to eight weeks in the field each year. Zoologists spend much of their time at a computer or on the telephone. Speaking of his daily activities, Dr. Gilmore says: "Getting up and starting with correspondence is, I think, number one. We communicate with colleagues all the time, and with the young people wanting to get into the field, and that's one thing we try to get out right away. We try to get letters and telephone calls returned. That's another thing. I think most people think they're going to be out in the boat, diving. No. You communicate. You communicate with the granting agencies, people that are going to support you. You communicate with the people that are going to work for you, or students. There's an awful lot of that going on. Part of my day—two or three hours—is devoted to that, and that alone. And then it's a joy to get to your data."

It is often the case that junior scientists spend more time in the field than do senior scientists, who study specimens and data collected in the field by their younger colleagues. Senior scientists spend much of their time coordinating research, directing younger scientists and technicians, and writing grant proposals or soliciting funds in other ways.

Raising money is an extremely important activity for zoologists who are not employed by government agencies or major universities. The process of obtaining money for research can be time-consuming and difficult. Dr. Gilmore, an expert fund-raiser, views it as the most difficult part of his job. Good development skills can also give scientists a flexibility that government-funded scientists do not have. Government money is sometimes available only for research into narrowly defined areas that may not be those that a scientist wishes to study. A zoologist who wants to study a particular area may seek his or her own funding in order not to be limited by governmental restrictions.

Requirements

A high school student who wants to prepare for a career in zoology should begin by making certain that he or she gets a well-rounded high school education. Although a solid grounding in biology and chemistry is an absolute necessity, the student should remember that facility in English will also be invaluable. Writing monographs and articles, communicating with colleagues both orally and in writing, and writing persuasive fund-raising proposals are all activities at which scientists need to excel. The student should also read widely, not merely relying on books on science or other subjects that are required by the school. The scientist-in-training should search the library for magazines and journals dealing with areas that are of interest to him or her. Developing the habit of reading will help prepare students for the days when they must keep up with the latest developments in the field while doing research and performing various other tasks. Computer skills are also essential, since most zoologists not only use the computer for writing, communication, and research, but also use various software packages to perform statistical analyses.

It's a good idea to look for internships. A student may, for example, spend a summer working at a scientific institution, at a zoo or aquarium, or on a research project, learning what the field is really like and making contacts that will be useful later on. Students should discuss the possibilities with their career counselors, but they should also read biological and other scientific publications and use the Internet to search for opportunities in their fields of interest. A student who is interested in marine biology, for example, should contact the Woods Hole Oceanographic Institute, the Scripps Institution of Oceanography, the Harbor Branch Oceanographic Institution, and as many other organizations as possible in the search for internships and other opportunities.

Dr. Gilmore recommends that college students who are interested in zoology avoid specializing at the undergraduate level: "I would say the best bet is to get a really good liberal arts degree and emphasize the sciences. If you're interested in biology, emphasize the biological sciences. And then, your graduate level is when you really make up your mind which direction you're going to go. But if you have the aptitude for the sciences, I think you should try a number of the different sciences. Just play the field when you can." Too many students specialize too soon and discover later that the field they have chosen is not the one for which they are best suited.

A bachelor's degree is essential for a zoologist, and advanced degrees are highly recommended, but no licensing or other certification is required, and there is no zoologists' union. Academic training, practical experience, and the ability to work effectively with others are the most important prerequisites for a career in zoology.

Success in zoology requires tremendous effort. It would be unwise for a person who wants to work an eight-hour day to become a zoologist, since hard work and long hours (sometimes sixty to eighty hours per week) are the norm. Also, although some top scientists are paid extremely well, the field does not provide a rapid route to riches. A successful zoologist finds satisfaction in work, not in a paycheck. The personal rewards, however, can be tremendous. The typical zoologist finds his or her work satisfying on many levels.

A successful zoologist is generally patient and flexible. A person who cannot juggle various tasks will have a difficult time in a job that requires doing research, writing articles, dealing with the public, teaching students, soliciting funds, and keeping up with the latest publications in the field. Flexibility also comes into play when funding for a particular area of study ends or is unavailable. A zoologist whose range of expertise is too narrowly focused will be at a disadvantage when there are no opportunities in that particular area. A flexible approach and a willingness to explore various areas can be crucial in such situations, and a too-rigid attitude may lead a zoologist to avoid studies that he or she would have found rewarding.

An aptitude for reading and writing is a must for any zoologist. A person who hates to read would have difficulty keeping up with the literature in the field, and a person who cannot write or dislikes writing would be unable to write effective articles and books. Publishing is an important part of zoological work, especially for those who are conducting research.

Opportunities for Experience and Exploration

One of the best ways to find out if you are suited for a career as a zoologist is to talk to zoologists and find out exactly what they do. Contact experts in your field of interest. If you are interested in birds, find out whether there is an ornithologist in your area. If there is not, find an expert in some other part of the country. Read books, magazines, and journals to find out who the experts are. Don't be afraid to write or call people and ask them questions.

One good way to meet experts is to attend meetings of professional organizations. If you are interested in fish, locate organizations of ichthyologists by searching in the library or on the Internet. If you can, attend an organization's meeting and introduce yourself to the attendees. Ask questions and learn as much as you can.

Try to become an intern or a volunteer at an organization that is involved in an area that you find interesting. Most organizations have internships, and if you look with determination for an internship, you are likely to find one.

Methods of Entering

Before you get your first job as a zoologist, you will need to have at least a bachelor's degree. For the best results, you will need a master's degree. It is possible to find work with a bachelor's degree, but it is likely that you will need to continue your education to advance in the field. Competition for jobs among those who have doctorate degrees is fierce, and it is often easier to break into the field with a master's than it is with a Ph.D. For this reason, many people go to work after they receive a master's degree and get a doctoral while they are working.

According to Dr. Gilmore, the best way to get your first job in zoology is "to make contacts. Make as many personal contacts as possible. And try to get a qualified scientist to help you out with that—someone who really knows the field and knows other people. If your adviser doesn't, try to find one who does. It's so competitive right now that the personal contact really makes a difference."

You will be ahead of the game if you have made contacts as an intern or as a member of a professional organization. It is an excellent idea to attend the meetings of professional organizations, which generally welcome students. At those meetings, introduce yourself to the scientists you admire and ask for their help and advice. Dr. Gilmore says, "I see too many students these days hesitating to go up to that renowned scientist and talk to him. Just go up and carry on a conversation. They seem to be afraid to do that. I think that's a big mistake."

Don't be shy, but be sure to treat people with respect. Ultimately, it's the way you relate to other people that determines how your career will develop. Says Gilmore, "I don't care what GPA you have. I don't care what SAT score you have or GRE score you have. That does not make one bit of difference. Everybody has high scores these days. It's the way you present yourself, your interests, the way you act. And that personal contact that makes all the difference."

Advancement

Higher education and publishing are two of the most important means of advancing in the field of zoology. The holder of a Ph.D. will make more money and have a higher status than the holder of a bachelor's or master's degree. The publication of articles and books is important for both research scientists and professors of zoology. A young professor who does not publish cannot expect to become a full professor with tenure, and a research scientist who does not publish the results of his or her research will not become known as an authority in the field. In addition, the publication of significant work lets everyone in the field know that the author has worked hard and accomplished something worthwhile.

Because zoology is not a career in which people typically move from job to job, people generally move up within an organization. A professor may become a full professor; a research scientist may become known as an expert in the field or may become the head of a department, division, or institution; a zoologist employed by an aquarium or a zoo may become an administrator or head curator. In some cases, however, scientists may not want what appears to be a more prestigious position. A zoologist who loves to conduct and coordinate research, for example, may not want to become an administrator who is responsible for budgeting, hiring and firing, and other tasks that have nothing to do with research.

Employment Outlook

According to the 1998-1999 edition of the *Occupational Outlook Handbook*, published by the U.S. Department of Labor, the significant job growth that the field of zoology (and other fields of biology) experienced from the 1980s to the middle 1990s has slowed. There are still jobs available, but competition for good positions—especially research positions—is increasing. Much of the decrease in growth has been caused by government budget cuts. It is expected, however, that growth will increase in the early twenty-first century, spurred partly by the need to analyze and offset the effects of pollution on the environment.

Those who are most successful in the field in the future are likely to be those who are able to diversify. Dr. Gilmore, who believes that the need for well-trained zoologists will increase in the next century, advises those entering the field to stay open-minded, maintain a wide range of contacts, and keep an eye out for what is occurring in related fields: "This is a danger in science today. People become so narrowly focused that it endangers their future. There's an ecological concept which I like to use that says 'Diversity is stability.' If you put all your marbles in one basket and somebody tips that basket, you're done for. Keep an open mind and keep open contacts."

Earnings

A study conducted by the National Association of Colleges and Employers determined that beginning salaries in private industry in 1997 averaged $25,400 for holders of bachelor's degrees in biological science (including zoologists), $26,900 for those with master's degrees, and $52,400 for holders of doctoral degrees.

According to the *Occupational Outlook Handbook*, the median annual wage for biological scientists in 1996 was $36,300, with the middle 10 percent earning between $28,400 and $50,900. The bottom 10 percent earned less than $22,000, while the top 10 percent made more than $66,000. In

1997, general biological scientists employed by the federal government earned an average salary of $52,100.

It is possible for the best and brightest of zoologists to make substantial amounts of money. Occasionally, a newly minted Ph.D. who has a top reputation may be offered a position that pays $80,000 or more per year, but only a few people begin their careers at such a high level.

The benefits that zoologists receive as part of their employment vary widely. Employees of the federal government or top universities tend to have extensive benefit packages, but the benefits offered by private industry cover a wide range, from extremely generous to almost nonexistent.

Conditions of Work

There is much variation in the conditions under which zoologists work. Professors of zoology may teach exclusively during the school year or may both teach and conduct research. Many professors whose school year consists of teaching spend their summers doing research. Research scientists spend some time in the field, but most of their work is done in the laboratory. There are zoologists who spend most of their time in the field, but they are the exceptions to the rule.

Zoologists who do field work may have to deal with difficult conditions. A gorilla expert may have to spend her time in the forests of Rwanda; a shark expert may need to observe his subjects from a shark cage. For most people in the field, however, that aspect of the work is particularly interesting and satisfying.

Zoologists spend much of their time corresponding with others in their field, studying the latest literature, reviewing articles written by their peers, and making and returning phone calls. They also log many hours working with computers, using computer modeling, performing statistical analyses, recording the results of their research, or writing articles and grant proposals.

No zoologist works in a vacuum. Even those who spend much time in the field have to keep up with developments within their specialty. In most cases, zoologists deal with many different kinds of people, including students, mentors, the public, colleagues, representatives of granting agencies, private or corporate donors, reporters, and science writers. For this reason, the most successful members of the profession tend to develop good communication skills.

Sources of Additional Information

The following society (formerly the American Society of Zoologists), which publishes the bimonthly journal American Zoologist, *is probably the best single source of information about all areas and aspects of zoology.*

Society for Integrative and Comparative Biology
401 North Michigan Avenue
Chicago, IL 60611-4267
Tel: 312-527-6697 or 800-955-1236
Email: sicb@sba.com
WWW: http://www.sicb.org

The following organization is an excellent source of information about zoological activities and organizations. It is a good place to look for schools, internships, and job opportunities.

American Institute of Biological Sciences
1444 Eye Street, NW, Suite 200
Washington, DC 20005
Tel: 202-628-1500
WWW: http://www.aibs.org

Index

t trainers, 3, 32-33, 35, 51-61, 63, 65-67, 70, 106

v veterinarians, 1-2, 4, 21, 34, 41, 46, 69, 96-97, 99, 111, **121-127**, 129-132, 145, 159
veterinary assistants, 2, 23, 129
veterinary technicians, 4, 43, 66-67, 70, 98, **129-135**
volunteers, 2, 26-28, 34-35, 40, 44-45, 52, 57, 68, 78-80, 99, 109, 115, 124, 132, 143, 149-150, 152, 161, 163, 174

W wildlife assistants, 23
wildlife biologists, 3-4, 73
wildlife conservationists, 3-4, 73
wildlife managers, 3-4, 73, 82
wildlife shelter workers, 23

Z zoo and aquarium curators, 4, **137-146**, 148
zoo and aquarium directors, 4, **147-155**
zoo directors, 1, 144
zoo veterinary technicians, 130, 133-135
zookeepers, 5, 139, 143, **157-168**
zoologists, 5, 161, **169-178**